"What a good subject to write a book about! The topic of the second chapter—how selective universities are usually the most affordable option for low-income students—is particularly important, as it is often ignored or looked at with disbelief." —**Jorge Domínguez**, Antonio Madero Professor for the Study of Mexico in the Department of Government and Chair of The Harvard Academy for International and Area Studies at Harvard University

"I'm always encouraging my students to aim high and apply to Ivy League schools, but reading a firsthand account will provide them with the guidance they need to get there. This book can help me guide students into creating a better future for themselves and their families." —**Anabel Basualdo**, Teacher of the Year, International Studies Charter High School

"*Achieve the College Dream: You Don't Need to Be Rich to Attend a Top School* addresses the unique and urgent concerns of a population of students who are largely underrepresented at our country's most selective colleges. This book is clearly and powerfully written. It is both a terrific tool and an inspiring story. It is comprehensive and from the heart. I have been waiting for a book like this for a long time. I wish I could give a copy of this book to every one of my students!" —**Joshua Steckel**, College Counselor, NYC Department of Education; coauthor, *Hold Fast to Dreams*

ACHIEVE THE COLLEGE DREAM

You Don't Need to Be Rich to Attend a Top School

María Carla Chicuén

ROWMAN & LITTLEFIELD
Lanham • Boulder • New York • London

Published by Rowman & Littlefield
A wholly owned subsidiary of The Rowman & Littlefield Publishing Group,
Inc.
4501 Forbes Boulevard, Suite 200, Lanham, Maryland 20706
www.rowman.com

Unit A, Whitacre Mews, 26-34 Stannary Street, London SE11 4AB

British Library Cataloguing in Publication Information Available

Library of Congress Cataloging-in-Publication Data

Names: Chicuén, María Carla, 1988– author.
Title: Achieve the college dream : you don't need to be rich to attend a top school / María Carla
     Chicuén.
Description: Lanham : Rowman & Littlefield, [2016] | Includes index.
Identifiers: LCCN 2016002276 | ISBN 9781475827347 (cloth: alk. paper)
Subjects: LCSH: Universities and colleges—United States—Admission. | Education, Higher—
     United States—Finance. | Minorities—Education (Higher)—United States.
Classification: LCC LB2351.2 .C48 2016 | DDC 378.1610973—dc23 LC record available at http://
     lccn.loc.gov/2016002276
     ISBN 978-0-8108-9493-8 (pbc: alk. paper)

∞ ™ The paper used in this publication meets the minimum requirements of
American National Standard for Information Sciences Permanence of Paper
for Printed Library Materials, ANSI/NISO Z39.48-1992.

Printed in the United States of America

In loving memory of Salvador Vicente Jr.
for the inspiration to achieve despite adversity

CONTENTS

FOREWORD

Education is a gift that once given, can never be taken away. It is a gift, however, that requires investment and participation on the part of the recipient. America is an amazing land of opportunity, one in which hard work and determination can open many doors.

Young people often don't focus on the future until they are about to graduate and then it can be difficult to get into the most prestigious colleges and universities if they haven't prepared properly—either because they didn't know what to do or didn't believe they could ever afford to go to an elite college.

I am often asked to give advice to students. I tell them that there are two parallel mistakes they can make about the future. The first is that they fail to consider the future. Too many young people live just for the moment, without regard for tomorrow. Tomorrow will come and so it is critical to understand that the choices they make today are important.

Think carefully about what courses are selected in high school. Opt for academically challenging classes that will serve as good preparation for the rigors of university work. Students should also gain leadership experience where possible by engaging in extracurricular activities and community service; all of which are attractive to admissions officers.

The second mistake students make, particularly those who come from low income and/or immigrant backgrounds, is to live in fear of the future, believing that their current situation will dictate what they can achieve tomorrow. Fear of the future, fear of the unknown, fear of the uncontrollable are all constricting forces that if left unchecked conspire to limit potential. They will keep you from deliberately and rationally moving forward. More importantly, they will keep you from actually enjoying life to its fullest. Do not be afraid of the future; instead, embrace it and prepare for it.

As educators, we strive to give our students the gift of education. To empower them to be independent thinkers, to be bold and believe in the possibilities that can become reality with hard work, determination and preparation. The resources and opportunities are out there if they are wise enough and willing to work for them. María Carla Chicuén is an example of what can be achieved when you set your sights on a goal and never look back.

"To dream the impossible dream" is not only a lyric from *Man of La Mancha*, it is the lesson learned by the author, who dreamed of going to an Ivy League university even though she once thought everything was stacked against her: meager income, language barrier, and immigrant background. But in this inspiring and practical guide for students, parents, and educators, she illustrates that not only is attending a school such as Harvard a laudable goal for any student, it can be attainable regardless of financial means or circumstance.

Beyond the practical steps that she outlines in *Achieve the College Dream*, María inspires us to look beyond the misperceptions and misconceptions that aiming for higher education may often throw in the way of those who think that the Ivy League is out of reach. She shows us that for those who truly want to go, they can get there. The trick is to start early and be persistent. The road isn't easy; it's not a limousine ride to Yale or Stanford, and nothing will be handed to you without working for it. But with drive and passion to better yourself, the kind of drive and passion exhibited by María, the sky is the limit.

This book provides hope, guidance, and a pathway to the dream and practical advice to make it come true. The future is what you make it.

Alberto M. Carvalho, Superintendent of Schools
Miami-Dade County Public Schools

ACKNOWLEDGMENTS

Writing this guide required a special mix of information and inspiration, the same essential ingredients of my transformative journey to college. Along the way, many people generously offered me the knowledge and encouragement that proved vital for the publication of my very first book.

I am indebted to Trevor and Chini, who made sure it all made sense; to Manuel, Eniko, Toby and Anabel, who provided insightful commentary; to Marta Isabel, Debora, Sheyla, Lucas and Ana Karla, who validated my purpose; to Shiv, Alex, Francis, Caroline and Nancy, who shed light on the book's possibilities; to Dina, who guided me through the publishing process; to David, Ms. Collins and Ms. G, who believed in me; to Jorge, who advised me always; to Sarah, from Rowman & Littlefield, who gave me the opportunity to bring this book to the world; to Emily, who introduced me to my wonderful agent, Lindsay, from Levine, Greenberg, Rostan; and to Lindsay, for her expert, tireless advocacy.

It is only fitting that my first book would spring from the nourishing sounds and smells of a coffee shop. I'm deeply thankful to the staff at Espresso Americano for letting me take over "my" table every morning during an unforgettable year in Panama.

This rewarding journey would not have been possible without the support and motivation of my family. To my parents and sister, who have been with me through it all; to my grandparents, aunts, uncles, and cousins, because it truly takes a village; and to my love, always by my side, thank you.

INTRODUCTION
Trust Me: It's Possible

The bell was about to ring when Ms. G, my English teacher, suddenly asked me to leave the classroom and join her for a brief conversation in the long, empty hallway. She looked at me directly in the eyes, grabbed my shoulders, and said firmly, "I know you are still a freshman, but you have to start thinking about your plans beyond high school. You might not think it's possible, but you could really end up studying at one of the best colleges in the country. Chase this opportunity. You might even get into Yale."

I thought Ms. G had gone completely mad. In my mind, a successful applicant to a selective university like Yale had to be either a true genius or a millionaire. I was far from either. As a recent immigrant from Cuba, I was struggling to learn English and the school counselors would not allow me to enroll in advanced subjects. While some of my classmates were already taking college-level courses I was stuck with regular English and basic ninth-grade math and science.

I was convinced that I didn't have what it takes to get into the kind of universities Ms. G was encouraging me to consider. And even if I did, I had heard that those schools charged students thousands of dollars every year. There was no way my parents would be able to afford even just a year of studies at any of them. My mother was unemployed, my dad worked multiple minimum-wage jobs to support the whole family, and my younger sister and I were free-lunch students at large public schools in South Florida.

When I was in high school, I didn't realize that selective colleges actually accept (and even actively seek!) low-income students, aiming to make their student bodies more diverse. As this book will explain in greater detail, many universities offer very generous financial aid to help families that cannot afford an expensive education. Some universities even charge students *only* what they can pay, and do not give preference to wealthier students in their evaluation for admission. The challenge for these schools is to spread the word among the students who could benefit from this financial aid, and convince them to apply.

My high school self thought, "Why bother?" Why risk getting rejected and adding the bitter feeling of failure to a life in which I already faced struggle? Or, even worse, what if I get accepted to one of these colleges against all odds and then have to decline the offer of admission because I cannot pay the elevated costs of attendance?

My family situation seemed too distant from the images of students in beautiful campus yards, high-tech classrooms, and sophisticated laboratories advertised in college brochures. Just a few months before, my mother, my sister, and I had moved to the United States from Cuba, our native country. My father had made the journey two years earlier, seeking work and stability to prepare for our arrival.

As soon as he received the news that we had finally secured permission to exit Cuba, he had left the room he was renting at the home of a Colombian family and found a small two-bedroom apartment where we could all settle more comfortably. We would live in Boynton Beach, a city about two hours north of Miami where my dad had secured employment as a drawbridge technician.

So far this was the closest he had gotten to a professional job. Since arriving in Florida, he had worked at a store selling Christmas trees, at a construction company doing accounting work, as an electrician installing pipes and cables in landfills full of rodents, at a cement factory, at an alarms company, and in several construction projects.

During most of his time in Florida, he had packed many of these jobs into single eighty-hour workweeks. This was in the early 2000s, a period of economic recession when few jobs were available even at McDonald's. My dad's plan was to certify his university degree in engineering as soon as he could, which might give him access to more professional opportunities and greater salaries. But the certification exams required time and money, neither of which he could spare at the moment.

As for my mother, she, like my sister and me, was an illegal immigrant, and couldn't get a work permit. Her only choices were informal jobs such as cleaning other people's houses or babysitting at a local gym. We hoped that someday she could return to her work as a pediatrician, a profession she loved and had exercised in Cuba for over twenty years. But in order to certify her medical degree in the United States she first needed to pass the incredibly difficult and expensive board exams and complete a residency program at a U.S. hospital. This, in turn, required learning English and revisiting scientific content she had not studied since her college years.

The modest savings we had brought from Cuba were pretty much spent during our first months in the United States. Aside from the expenses associated with my mother's test preparation, we needed basic furniture and appliances for the new apartment, as well as school uniforms and supplies. We also had to pay for several required vaccines and medical checkups. And we needed clothes, since we had left most behind. Generous friends and family helped us meet these burdening costs or donated some of their own belongings, easing our transition into our new country and our new life.

Among all the new sights I absorbed during my first few weeks in the United States, one in particular caught my attention: the campus of the local Florida International University (FIU). I was driving around Miami with my dad, running some errands, and he made it a point to stop by the entrance of University Park, the main FIU campus. "*Tata*, this could be your future college. Isn't it nice?" I remember thinking it was nice, with its lush vegetation, surrounding lakes, and modern white buildings. Right then, it suddenly struck me that in just a few years I could choose among many universities, old and modern, and not only in Florida, but all throughout the United States and even the world. Yet, I still wasn't sure that top U.S. colleges were actually a possibility.

My doubts reflected a general understanding that selective U.S. colleges are inaccessible, especially for high school students with few economic resources. It's a known fact that most low-income students with high grades and test scores—two of the most important admissions criteria—do not apply to any selective colleges. What many don't know is that the talented low-income students who do apply are very likely to be admitted *and* to graduate at high rates. At the same time, thanks to selective colleges' generous financial aid policies, these institutions generally cost low-income students less than the nonselective institutions to which these students normally choose to apply.[1]

The first sign that perhaps, just perhaps, selective colleges were not as unreachable as I thought came toward the end of ninth grade, when I read that four graduates of the nearby Hialeah High School had started college at Harvard the year before. Incredibly, two more students from the school's 2003 senior class had just been accepted to Harvard. I could hardly believe it. These two students were recent Cuban immigrants like me, and they had also learned English just a few years before.

I was floored. I was familiar with the Hialeah community, a residential area where many Hispanic families, usually of limited means, would settle upon arrival in the United States. I also knew some people who attended Hialeah High, and had heard that only about half of the school's graduates enrolled in college. How was it possible that this same school was now sending a disproportionate number of graduates to Harvard two years in a row? Even more baffling, how could these surely low-income recent immigrants afford a university with annual costs of over $50,000?

During a visit to South Florida that year, the president of Harvard at the time, Lawrence Summers, explained that Harvard University was open to any student regardless of their family's financial position. In his own words, "no one should hesitate to apply to Harvard because they think they won't be able to afford to come."[2]

Summers' message motivated me to explore Harvard's official website and check the costs of attendance. What I learned left me in awe. It turns out that in early 2004 Harvard had launched a Financial Aid Initiative (HFAI) to make college education affordable for all families. At the time, Summers had commented that "Harvard is open to talented students from all economic backgrounds. . . . Too often, outstanding students from families of modest means do not believe that college is an option for them—much less an Ivy League university."[3]

According to its admissions website, Harvard accepted students based on their academic, extracurricular, and personal qualities; the student or family's ability to pay the costs of attendance was not taken into consideration. This admissions policy was called "need-blind," and helped me clear many of my doubts about elite universities. For example, I believed that students from very rich families were pretty much guaranteed acceptance at these universities. I also believed that even the most talented students could not study at Harvard and other selective institutions unless they could pay the full costs. I had no clue about the increasingly generous financial aid offered by these universities, or their tendency to reduce the students' costs of attendance through scholarships based more on the economic need of the family than on the students' academic and extracurricular merits.

As I continued my research on the affordability of top U.S. colleges, I realized that Harvard was not the only university offering very generous financial aid options to low-income students. Starting in 2001, Princeton University pioneered the "no-loan" policy among U.S. universities, by which low-income students receive grants that do not have to be repaid.[4] Like Harvard, Princeton does not offer scholarships for academic or athletic merits; its financial aid depends on the family's ability to pay the costs of attendance.

In March 2005, Yale also announced a policy that allowed students with family incomes less than $45,000 per year to attend Yale College at no cost.[5] Other top universities such as Stanford, Brown, Columbia, and the University of Pennsylvania soon followed with their own policies to reduce the financial burden of students from low-income families.

As I advanced through high school I continued researching selective universities' financial aid policies, becoming more and more aware that low-income students could afford to attend top colleges offering generous financial aid packages. But could we actually get in? Was it worth applying? A hint toward the answers arrived by post during my junior year. In our mailbox, my mother found a small envelope bearing a crimson shield. It was a letter from Harvard. And it was addressed to me.

I remember opening the envelope with shaky hands and reading the impossible news. Two current Harvard students were writing to congratulate me on my academic achievements (how could they know?) and to encourage me to consider Harvard as an option to pursue college studies.

The letter described Harvard's vibrant academic and extracurricular resources. It mentioned the wide range of disciplines in which students could major or minor, the outstanding faculty, the internship and research opportunities, and the incredibly diverse student body. I learned that there were over four hundred student-led extracurricular organizations in many areas such as the arts, sports, and others I hadn't even considered. Suddenly, a university like Harvard seemed more real than ever.

Besides Harvard, what most appealed to me about many of the top colleges was the possibility to obtain a high-quality education that was also affordable. As I began to explore non-selective institutions with lower costs of attendance, I realized that many were more expensive in practice because their financial aid was significantly less generous and most of it was awarded on the basis of academic merit rather than economic need.

It became apparent to me that greater selectivity was not a sign of greater cost. As I saw it, I only had two realistic choices regarding higher studies: I could either attend one of the top colleges with the help of their scholarships or I would have to settle for a local university or community college with a very low sticker price.

Tip: The "sticker price" is the full cost of attendance usually published on each college's official website. The "net price" is the sticker price minus the financial aid received by a student. Therefore, the "net price" is what the student will actually have to pay and it is much more important than the sticker price. Due to financial aid, a university with a higher sticker price can be many times cheaper than another apparently less costly school.

Motivated by all this new knowledge, I armed myself with confidence during my senior year and decided to dream big, following my English teacher's advice. Looking back, I am so grateful that I overcame my fears about the accessibility of selective colleges and submitted applications to the local University of Miami and University of Florida, but also to Harvard, Princeton, Columbia, Dartmouth, Yale, and the University of Pennsylvania. All but Yale accepted me.

A year later, when I finally arrived at Harvard, it felt like a dream when I met the same students from Hialeah High who had first inspired my research on selective colleges. I could not have anticipated that we would all belong to the same salsa dance group! And little did I know that in a similarly magical turn of events, I would soon be writing to prospective students the same encouraging letter I had received in my own mailbox. From my post as recruiter at the Harvard College Admissions and Financial Aid Office for three years, I communicated to thousands of students and their families that top colleges were not only affordable, but also accessible, for students who could demonstrate outstanding academic skills, civic promise, and noble character.

In this book I seek to share the message with an even wider audience. I hope that my advice and personal experiences spark the interest of parents, teachers, guidance counselors, and students, motivating readers to identify and nurture the potential of every young person they may encounter. Although the book mainly targets high school students and their parents, the content can be also be useful for those in middle school. Besides my specific tips on how to choose the best high schools or how to craft an appealing academic curriculum as early as sixth grade, middle school students will benefit from the general awareness about the opportunities that await them at selective colleges, and what they can do already to secure them.

It would be wonderful if every reader—whether a parent, teacher, counselor, or student—would turn the last page of the book convinced that the finest education in the country is within reach.

1

A COLLEGE EDUCATION

The Path to Prosperity and Opportunity

In the United States, one single decision has the potential to enable *any* person to reach the American Dream. This decision leads to greater earnings throughout one's lifetime, increases economic opportunities for one's children, reduces the likelihood of unemployment, and even improves individual health. Yes, this decision is to attend college and acquire a bachelor's degree.

A college education is, without exaggeration, the most effective path to prosperity in this country. In 2013, the average U.S. college graduate made 98 percent more per hour than non-college graduates. That year the pay gap between college graduates and individuals without a college degree reached a record high.[1] People who attend college earn wages that are over $20,000 higher on average than those of people with just a high school diploma. They also tend to see their salaries rise more rapidly over time than the earnings of less educated workers.[2]

The benefits of a college education also extend into other areas of a person's life. For example, college graduates are more likely to receive health insurance and pension benefits from employers and to spend less on health care.[3] Going to college decreases the likelihood of future unemployment as well. As technology advances and professional careers evolve, it is predicted that more jobs will increasingly require a college education. In 2018, over half of the jobs in the arts, design, entertainment, sports, and media, just to name a few areas, will require at least a bachelor's degree.[4]

For people from low-income backgrounds, a college education offers even greater benefits. Someone at the bottom of the income distribution without a college degree has only a 55 percent chance of moving to higher income quartiles. Give that person a college degree and suddenly the chances of making it out of the bottom increase to 84 percent.[5]

The benefits associated with a bachelor's degree increase when individuals attend a top college. On the one hand, attending top colleges translates into greater professional opportunities because these institutions provide better education, more effective career counseling, access to a powerful and supportive alumni network, and internships that enable students to acquire valuable skills even before they enter the workforce as full-time employees. Top colleges also attract potential employers directly, many of which promote their vacancies and recruit students on campus on a regular basis.[6]

Another advantage of attending selective institutions is associated with graduation rates. A high graduation rate is a sign of the school's quality and its overall ability to facilitate students' education and transition to higher academic levels. The great majority of students from low-income backgrounds at the nation's 146 most selective colleges graduate within six years, versus just over half of equally achieving students at non-selective institutions.[7] This disparity reflects the support structures available at selective colleges to ensure successful completion of the undergraduate program.

At selective colleges, processes such as enrollment, course selection, and a change in academic major are easier to navigate because there is less bureaucracy. Tutors are readily available to help students struggling with academics. Other staff also provides coaching on a wide range of critical skills such as time-management, exam-taking strategies, focus and concentration, coping with learning disorders, effective collaboration, language learning, and even memory improvement.

The value of the resources that a college provides each student is a strong indicator of the financial return of an undergraduate education. It is estimated that the most selective colleges in the United States invest $92,000 per student, whereas the least selective schools spend only $12,000.[8] This difference explains why selective colleges are most likely to provide a quality, integral education that includes the following elements:

- Renowned and experienced professors
- Research centers and databases
- State-of-the-art facilities such as dorms, libraries, laboratories, and gyms
- Campus-based student health services
- Counseling (i.e., career planning, academic tutoring, and wellness advice)
- Co-curricular opportunities (i.e., study abroad programs and field work)
- Diversity of academic majors, minors, and courses
- Committed, influential, and widespread alumni networks
- Extracurricular opportunities, including student-run organizations
- Funding to pursue individual academic and extracurricular projects

Given the strong relationship between a college education and success in so many important areas of life, students with limited resources who want to increase their personal, academic, and professional opportunities would thus do well to consider a bachelor's degree as a requirement, not an option.

Within my family, obtaining a university degree was never presented as a choice. I was exceptionally lucky because my parents always cultivated in my sister and me deep admiration for academic and professional achievement. As I grew up, my parents would repeat again and again that education was an investment that would always yield returns. They convinced us that knowledge was the one thing in life nobody could take away from you. Money, properties, even loved ones could disappear. But not knowledge.

This thinking had acquired greater meaning in our new context as recent immigrants facing significant scarcity. In these circumstances, the promise of a better life depended on my parents' ability to exercise their professions in the United States and in the education my sister and I could obtain. There seemed to be no American Dream without a college degree.

GOING TO COLLEGE VS. GETTING A JOB

Despite the evidence that college is the ultimate bridge to progress in the United States, some people still challenge the importance of an undergraduate education. Students in low-income communities are especially vulnerable to this influence because they might see college as an unaffordable luxury rather than a manageable investment (although, as will be explained in the next chapter, it is possible for low-income students to attend even the most expensive colleges in the country at no cost at all).

For example, some people will say that time spent in college could instead be dedicated to a full-time job that would allow them to start earning money. High school students can fall for this shortsighted thinking if they are unaware of the impressive long-term financial benefits of a college education and the opportunity to work throughout the college years in exchange for substantial salaries later on.

Indeed, many college students hold jobs on campus throughout the academic year at places as varied as libraries, coffee shops, research centers, and administration offices. University employers provide unmatched flexibility, ensuring that working hours do not interfere with the students' coursework or extracurricular activities.

I personally had several jobs throughout college. Before I became a minority recruiter for the Harvard College Admissions & Financial Aid Office, I had already been working as a Spanish translator and interpreter for Harvard's student-run translation agency. I also participated in the freshman orientation employment program hosted by Dorm Crew, the campus cleaning services.

Like Harvard, most universities offer diverse and flexible employment opportunities to current students. As a freshman at Stanford University, my younger sister accepted her first part-time job at the sports and recreation center on campus. In exchange for ten hours of work as student social media manager, every week my sister received a salary that allowed her to cover her personal expenses. Campus jobs usually offer the chance to gain promotions and receive salary increases, with some full-time students earning as much as $20,000 a year.

Colleges, especially the most selective ones, also facilitate gainful employment during break periods. Students often receive grants from the university itself to work at a wide variety of organizations. Some students even obtain very lucrative positions in fields like management consulting or finance during the summer months, after meeting their employers on campus at job fairs organized by the university. Given their resources and prestige, selective institutions are uniquely able to offer students this wide range of quality employment opportunities. Top employers also trust the ability of selective universities to generate a greater pool of promising candidates given these institutions' rigorous admissions criteria and academic preparation.

THE IMPORTANCE OF COLLEGE VS. GRADUATE SCHOOL

High school students looking beyond college and planning to acquire a graduate degree might also encounter people who will deem college unimportant relative to graduate studies. Many students are advised to relax and just remember that where they are going to college doesn't really matter. They are told that college is a rather inconsequential bridge connecting high school and graduate school—the real indicator and determinant of success. Therefore, if one were to invest, financially and otherwise, in higher education, one should do so in graduate rather than undergraduate schooling.

This kind of college skeptic ignores the fact that attending a selective undergraduate program increases a person's chances of both applying and being admitted to graduate school. The Jack Kent Cook Foundation reports that 35 percent of graduates from the most selective universities go on to pursue graduate degrees, compared to the 21 percent national average.[9] One reason for this may be that selective colleges tend to offer a better curriculum, preparing students more effectively to tackle the increased academic rigor at the graduate level. At the same time, the fact that selective colleges send more students to graduate school means that current students have a wider network of alumni role models who can provide guidance on the transition.

Beyond the academic and professional relationships, people who challenge the inherent importance of a college education also ignore the value of the social relationships that are unique to this life period. In college, especially at selective institutions that promote on-campus housing, students spend about four years in very tight communities.

They bond through classes, but also over meals, extracurricular activities, homework sessions, part-time jobs, and campus-wide events. The regularity and intensity of these common experiences help cultivate lifelong friendships with peers regardless of their background.

> Although I have a master's degree, which has served me a great deal, there is no doubt that my college experience was far more enriching. College allowed me to share a dorm with four wonderful roommates, each from a different cultural heritage. College also funded my trips to over ten countries, where I conducted academic research, took part in exciting internships, led international conferences, or simply wandered. College required me to develop critical thinking and writing abilities, which have turned out to be my most applicable professional skills.
>
> Sadly, there are teachers, friends, and family members who discourage students from pursuing these opportunities, warning them that they "won't fit in." When I told my great-uncle that I had accepted Harvard's admissions offer, for example, he immediately expressed disapproval and told me that Harvard was a place for rich people where I would not be welcomed. He also offered to send along the names of a few colleges that could surely provide a more comfortable environment for someone with limited means.
>
> While I'm sure my great-uncle meant well, he had an outdated viewpoint. When he moved to the United States in the early 1960s, colleges were just beginning to diversify their student populations, moving away from the predominance of white males from middle or upper-income families. Back then, need-based financial aid was just emerging, aided by the passage of the 1965 Higher Education Act, and prevailing attitudes in higher education discriminated against women, ethnic minorities and the poor.

Today, the United States is more diverse than ever, and universities increasingly reflect this plurality of racial, ethnic, and socioeconomic backgrounds. At selective universities, though not as often as it should occur, the sons and daughters of high government officials and millionaire executives share dorms with those of illegal immigrants and domestic workers. Their differences often pale in comparison with the passion for learning and motivation that unites them, and they soon realize that they thrive in diverse and intellectually stimulating environments that attract people who *inspire* them, no matter their origin. This is the kind of experience that colleges are especially poised to offer. And, contrary to what many believe, this experience can be affordable.

2

SELECTIVE COLLEGES

A Most Affordable Option for Low-Income Students

Over the last few decades, universities in the United States have made significant efforts to diversify student communities along socioeconomic, ethnic, racial, and gender lines. Among these efforts, the initiative to attract students from the poorest sectors of society is of crucial importance not only for individual students and universities, but also for the country at large. The U.S. government recognizes that national economic growth and the expansion of the middle class largely depend on educational attainment, especially at the university level. Over the last forty years the share of jobs requiring postsecondary education has doubled,[1] making college access a necessity to combat unemployment.

Many top universities are implementing initiatives that ensure every student can afford its tuition and all the resources available on campus, while most schools see attracting a diverse student body as an increasing priority. More and more, diversity is being understood as an essential component of the learning process, and globalization has created additional pressures to ensure diversity in the university environment. In today's interconnected world, graduates are likely to live and work in different countries, and their colleagues will likely represent the wide range of backgrounds that exist all over the world. Therefore, college populations that represent this diverse landscape can more effectively provide students the awareness and tolerance to thrive in the workforce.

Students from the lowest-income families—those making $30,000 or less annually—make up more than 15 percent of the total number of students at more than a dozen of the most selective, highest-ranked U.S. colleges; this includes the Massachusetts Institute of Technology (MIT), Amherst, Wellesley, Stanford, and Dartmouth. The representation of these students at other top universities is more modest, but it has nonetheless stayed on the rise. At Yale, for example, it has increased from 10 percent in 2006 to 14 percent in 2013. At Princeton, the representation grew from 9 percent to 12 percent during the same period.[2]

Often, however, the fact that many students of very limited means attend these prestigious universities is met with looks of disbelief. The math doesn't seem to make sense. Many of these students' families are earning less than $30,000 each year, and yet they are sending their sons and daughters to schools that cost over $50,000 a year? The reason for this apparent paradox is that many selective universities require students to pay only what they can afford. Not a single cent more.

UNDERSTANDING WHAT MAKES TOP COLLEGES AFFORDABLE

In the United States, many selective colleges have actually become more affordable to low-income students than nonselective institutions. This has been made possible thanks to the implementation of the following financial aid policies at some of the most selective universities:

- *Need-blind admission.* According to this policy, the admissions committee evaluates applications without taking into consideration the applicant's economic status. Such policy ensures that the committee does not discriminate against students who cannot pay the full cost of attendance.
- *Need-based financial aid.* This means the university awards financial aid based primarily or exclusively on the economic status of the student, rather than the student's academic or extracurricular merits (merit-based aid). Thanks to this policy, the university ensures that its limited funds are allocated to the students that most need them.

- *Meeting full financial need.* This policy allows the university to pay the difference between the total cost of attendance and the maximum amount the student's family can pay. In other words, the student's family will pay only what it can. Meeting full financial need is a type of need-based financial aid.
- *No-loan policy.* Universities following this policy award financial aid in the form of grants, versus loans that require repayment.

There are a few dozen private selective colleges that meet the full financial need of low-income students from the United States.[3] This group includes six Ivy League institutions: Brown, Columbia, Harvard, Princeton, Yale, and the University of Pennsylvania. Other top universities such as Duke, Amherst, Hamilton, Reed, Vanderbilt, William & Mary, and, most recently, Northeastern, also claim to charge students only what they can afford.

To truly internalize that very expensive colleges are affordable, it is useful to look at what low-income students *actually* paid at some of the top colleges during the 2010–2011 academic year. At Amherst, the lowest-income students paid an average annual net price of just $448. At the California Institute of Technology, $310. At Harvard, $1,297. And, at Washington University in St. Louis, they paid $0![4]

These low individual costs are a reflection of incredibly generous financial aid policies at the nation's top colleges. At MIT, for example, 58 percent of undergraduates in the 2012–2013 academic year received a need-based scholarship averaging $33,697.[5] Princeton reports that its financial aid spending has grown by more than 150 percent since 2003, offering recipients an average grant of almost $40,000.[6]

Top universities are also more likely than their non-selective counterparts to provide low-income students a kind of financial aid that does not have to be repaid. In other words, these universities offer students grants, which are like gifts, instead of lending them money that has to be repaid with interest. As a result, low-income students that attend selective universities often graduate with no debt.

It is also important to keep in mind that selective institutions are able to provide financial support toward the full cost of attendance, not just tuition. This means that low-income students at most top colleges not only get to attend classes for free or for a very low cost, but they also receive a significant or complete subsidy toward the residential experience.

General financial aid packages for low-income students, for example, give them the chance to live in safe and comfortable student dorms, receive meals at dining halls, and take advantage of the support network available at student residences, which usually includes the presence of academic tutors, counselors, mentors, security guards, and administrative staff. Indeed, selective institutions allow students to complement the traditional academic experience with a wide range of opportunities for personal growth. They provide funding for students to spend time abroad, conduct academic research, pursue graduate school, receive academic and personal counseling, and even attend gym classes.

When I deliver presentations about the experience offered at selective universities, I usually illustrate the available academic and extracurricular opportunities through examples from my own time at Harvard. I mention that I lived with Hungarian, Portuguese, African-American, and Chinese-American roommates. That I met at least five presidents at Harvard's Institute of Politics. That on my twentieth birthday, the winner of the Nobel Prize for Literature, Mario Vargas Llosa, autographed my copy of *Conversation in the Cathedral* during his talk on campus. That Harvard gave me money to travel to Madrid and London one summer so that I could conduct research for my thesis. That I participated in debate conferences in Costa Rica, El Salvador, and Mexico. That my peers came from so many different countries that now I have at least one friend in every corner of the world. These experiences are not restricted to rich people.

WHY HARVARD MIGHT BE A STUDENT'S CHEAPEST OPTION

Contrary to common perception, the presence of such generous financial aid policies at selective institutions means that low-income students can actually face higher costs at non-selective schools. Given the more limited resources of less selective institutions, their wealth largely depends on tuition payments. As a result, even the non-selective schools in the student's city and state of residence might charge higher prices than top colleges, despite the availability of special financial aid for local residents.

By the time I submitted my college applications, I still couldn't get my head around the claim that the top schools could be more afford-able than less selective, lower-ranked universities located in my home state of Florida. It wasn't until I was admitted to the local University of Miami that I was able to confirm this fact. The University of Miami's financial aid is primarily based on students' merit rather than their economic need. In the 2010–2011 school year, this institution charged the lowest-income students (22 percent of its student body) an average of $21,415.[7]

During my senior year, Harvard's generous financial offer made the University of Miami a much more expensive college option for me. Given my family's low income, Harvard required us to pay just a very small fraction of its full attendance cost. Harvard even gave me additional money to purchase a laptop computer. I would later hear from my Harvard peers that they had also received similar financial aid packages, with some obtaining free winter coats and vouchers to attend campus events at no cost. I realized then that selective universities could offer not only a cheaper cost, but also a more affordable overall life experience.

Throughout my four years at Harvard, I never felt like I was missing out on any opportunity because of my low-income back-ground. I studied, worked, and conducted research abroad. My sala-ry from my part-time employment at the Admissions Office allowed me to cover my personal expenses and participate in a fun, fulfilling social life with my friends. I was involved in many extracurricular organizations and held numerous leadership positions. And I never suffered discrimination.

If many top universities offer a superior academic and extracurricu-lar experience, and if they are affordable, why don't low-income stu-dents apply for admission at the same rate they apply to the nonselec-tive universities that end up costing them a lot more? One reason for this "under-matching" is that many students wish to remain close to their families and apply only to local institutions regardless of their cost and selectivity. An even greater factor that explains the application be-havior of low-income high-achievers is lack of awareness.

Many students could benefit from the guidance of counselors, teachers, or family members knowledgeable about selective universities' admissions and financial aid policies. Without the advice of this support network, students might never hear that they could attend prestigious universities at little or no cost. Perhaps a greater concern is that they would never be accepted.

And yet, many talented low-income students don't realize that they already have what it takes to get into the nation's top colleges. As the next chapter will explain in detail, admissions offices at these colleges focus on a wide range of academic and non-academic factors to determine which applicants are strong candidates. Students might be surprised to learn that fulfilling these general requirements depends much more on focus and perseverance than on genius or wealth.

3

THE MEANING OF HIGH ACHIEVEMENT
What Admission Officers Are Looking For

Anybody who has been following college admissions news in recent years knows that there is widespread anxiety about what makes students good candidates for top U.S. colleges. Books, news articles, and blogs constantly reveal their "findings" about the mysterious formula, the one that seemingly determines which small percentage of applicants will receive the dreamed-of fat envelopes containing acceptance letters.

The existence of such formula is a misconception. Prospective students and their families should know that admissions officers at selective colleges do not evaluate applicants through a process of elimination (in which, for example, a candidate is immediately disqualified if certain defined criteria such as minimum test scores are not met). Instead, admissions officers at selective institutions conduct what they call a *holistic* evaluation of a prospective student's academic achievement, extracurricular engagement, and character.

THE "HOLISTIC" APPLICATION REVIEW

When admissions officers say they evaluate candidates "holistically" they mean that no single factor, whether academic or extracurricular, can guarantee a student's acceptance or rejection. In the same way that a student will not be admitted to selective universities on the basis of test scores alone, a student will not be rejected solely because the test scores are low compared to the scores of the average admitted student.

Admissions officers attempt to form a full picture of an applicant's academic, extracurricular, professional, and personal life, including the circumstances that shed light on why students made important decisions in each one of these areas. Universities will try to understand if, for example, the student had to face special challenges at school or at home that affected the student's academic performance, or the ability to participate in extracurricular activities. This kind of contextual background is as important to admissions officers as the student's academic and extracurricular credentials.

Differences in individual circumstances might explain why someone with just good grades gets into a very selective school, while the same school rejects another applicant with near perfect scores in the same classes or exams. Holistically, the first person might have been a much stronger applicant even if one aspect of this person's application was inferior compared to other applicants.

The purpose of this rigorous evaluation method is to form a class with unique talents and diverse backgrounds who will benefit from the institution's education and resources as much as they will enrich the college community and inspire one another's growth. Applicants, therefore, are not evaluated in isolation from the rest. On its official website MIT offers a helpful metaphor to illustrate how individual students are also assessed in terms of how they would fit within their class:

> When we admit a class of students to MIT, it's as if we're choosing a 1,000-person team to climb a very interesting, fairly rugged mountain—together. We obviously want people who have the training, stamina and passion for the climb. At the same time, we want each to add something useful or intriguing to the team, from a wonderful temperament or sense of humor, to compelling personal experiences, to a wide range of individual gifts, talents, interests and achievements. We are emphatically not looking for a batch of identical perfect climbers; we are looking for a richly varied team of capable people who will support, surprise and inspire each other.[1]

But how exactly does a university evaluate students? The website of the Harvard College Admissions & Financial Aid Office includes a series of specific questions considered by Harvard College admissions officers as they review each application. These questions are particularly helpful because they provide greater clarity about the "magical" selection criteria and because they also largely guide the evaluation of applicants at other top colleges. These are the questions:[2]

Growth and potential

- Have you reached your maximum academic and personal potential?
- Have you been stretching yourself?
- Have you been working to capacity in your academic pursuits, your full-time or part-time employment, or other areas?
- Do you have reserve power to do more?
- How have you used your time?
- Do you have initiative? Are you a self-starter? What motivates you?
- Do you have a direction yet? What is it? If not, are you exploring many things?
- Where will you be in one, five, or 25 years? Will you contribute something to those around you?
- What sort of human being are you now? What sort of human being will you be in the future?

Interests and activities

- Do you care deeply about anything—intellectual? Extracurricular? Personal?
- What have you learned from your interests? What have you done with your interests? How have you achieved results? With what success or failure? What have you learned as a result?
- In terms of extracurricular, athletic, community, or family commitments, have you taken full advantage of opportunities?
- What is the quality of your activities? Do you appear to have a genuine commitment or leadership role?

- If you have not had much time in high school for extracurricular pursuits due to familial, work, or other obligations, what do you hope to explore at Harvard with your additional free time?

Character and personality

- What choices have you made for yourself? Why?
- Are you a late bloomer?
- How open are you to new ideas and people?
- What about your maturity, character, leadership, self-confidence, warmth of personality, sense of humor, energy, concern for others, and grace under pressure?

Contribution to the Harvard community

- Will you be able to stand up to the pressures and freedoms of College life?
- Will you contribute something to Harvard and to your classmates? Will you benefit from your Harvard experience?
- Would other students want to room with you, share a meal, be in a seminar together, be teammates, or collaborate in a closely knit extracurricular group?

Source: https://college.harvard.edu/admissions/application-process /what-we-look

These questions reveal that admissions officers screen applicants' files for much more than academic aptitude. In every part of the application evaluators will look for cues into the *meaning* of each academic, extracurricular, and professional accomplishment. They will attempt to form, as accurately as possible, a vivid and complex picture of the person you are and the person you have the potential to become.

Certainly, the holistic evaluation process, which contrasts with misguided ideas about minimum acceptance requirements, might puzzle rather than appease students. How is it possible to measure things as intangible as character, initiative, maturity, or the temperature of one's personality? How could an admissions officer possibly know if one has reached one's full potential? And, given that admissions officers receive thousands of applications each year in a period of just a couple of months, how can they get to know each applicant well enough to conduct such a complex assessment?

Admissions officers try to answer these questions as accurately as possible through a series of metrics used to evaluate applicants in the three main categories described earlier: academic skills, extracurricular participation, and character.

Academic Skills

Even though universities (especially the most selective ones) offer a rich variety of experiences inside and outside of the classroom, they remain first and foremost institutions of learning. Therefore, their main admissions requirement is strong academic preparation and ability to excel in courses at the university level.

While admissions officers consider a range of indicators of academic competency, none is most important than sustained strong performance in a rigorous high school curriculum. The latter usually comprises the following minimum elements:

- Four years of English (including language and literature)
- Four years of mathematics (including pre-calculus and, ideally, calculus)
- Four years of science with a laboratory component (including biology, chemistry, and physics)
- Four years of social studies (including world history, U.S. history, European history, and U.S. government)
- Four years of a single foreign language

Admissions officers look favorably upon students who take these and other courses at a higher level—such as honors, Advanced Placement (AP), or International Baccalaureate (IB)—whenever this opportunity is available. Universities will take into consideration the school's academic offerings and will not penalize students for not taking AP classes if this type of course, for example, is not available at the school. However, as will be explained in the next chapter, universities will reward students who go out of their way to enrich their curriculum beyond what their school offers them.

In the context of selective admissions, a student's high school course history is as important as measurable success in the courses, as indicated by grades in the A or 90–100 range. This is why admissions officers also pay close attention to students' cumulative academic average, known as grade point average (GPA).

Knowing that individual course grades and cumulative average are important college admissions criteria, some students hesitate to enroll in advanced classes for fear that the increased rigor might hamper their ability to obtain high grades and thus a competitive GPA. This is a mistake that top students aspiring to attend the top colleges should not make. Even though the ideal applicant will present both a rigorous academic curriculum and high grades, what ultimately bears more weight in the admissions process is the student's readiness for college-level classes.

Advanced high school subjects, rather than regular ones, are more likely to deliver this preparation even when the student does not attain perfect grades. At the same time, prestigious colleges seek people who challenge themselves even when they aren't sure they can accomplish the task. Giving more rigorous classes a try will signal that the student prioritizes learning over grades, an attitude expected from college students as well.

Admissions officers also look at a student's place in the class rank as another measure of academic performance. Whereas the GPA indicates the extent to which a student has mastered academic material, the class rank, by definition, describes how a given student has performed academically relative to his peers. The most selective colleges usually seek students within the top 10 percent of their class.

Tip: Many students think that unless they become valedictorian or salutatorian—the titles respectively given to students who occupy the first and second place in the class rank—they will not be considered competitive applicants to top universities. Many valedictorians and salutatorians, however, do not make it into the most selective colleges, while their lower-ranked peers do. This is proof that colleges look at a student's overall qualities, and that grades and class rank alone do not determine admission.

It is worth noticing that schools often create their own formulas to calculate the GPA, so a 4.0 GPA at one high school might indicate a completely different relative performance than the same GPA value at another institution. For this reason, the GPA and class rank are not sufficient to compare applicants from different high schools, much less from different countries.

Standardized tests such as the SAT and ACT exams offer admissions officers an opportunity to assess the relative academic aptitude of applicants from all over the world, regardless of their schools of origin. This is why most selective universities require that students take at least one of these tests before submitting the application for admission. Usually, students accepted into the top universities score between 700 and 800 on each section of the SAT, and above thirty on the ACT. Chapter 8 will explain universities' testing requirements in more detail.

In recent years, standardized tests have been the subject of dispute as some research suggests there is no strong correlation between performance on these exams and success in college-level academics. Critics of the SAT and ACT also argue that the tests unjustly benefit students from higher income backgrounds with access to expensive test prep materials and tutors. As a result, some universities are beginning to pay less attention to standardized exams, with a few eliminating the requirement altogether. Most selective universities, however, still expect competitive applicants to obtain high scores in these tests.

Tip: On its official website, www.fairtest.org, the National Center for Fair and Open Testing offers an updated list of colleges that do not require the SAT or ACT exams or that use them only for placement and research purposes.

The fact that students with more economic resources are more likely to access expensive test prep and tutors should not discourage talented low-income students. Instead, they should recognize that there is an opportunity to stand out from other applicants by doing really well in the SAT or ACT. As the next chapter will describe, there are many ways to prepare for these exams for little or no cost.

To summarize, here are the criteria that college admissions officers take into consideration to evaluate a student's *academic* achievement:

- Rigor of the high school curriculum
- Final grades in individual subjects throughout high school
- Cumulative GPA
- Class rank
- Performance in standardized testing (ACT or SAT, and SAT Subject Test)

The set of criteria used by universities to evaluate applicants' readiness for college-level academics is by no means intended to measure a student's general knowledge or potential (hardly signaled by scores and grades alone). The world is ripe with highly intelligent people who, for a variety of reasons, do not obtain excellent grades during their years in high school. There are other people who exhibit extraordinary achievement in just one academic or professional area. Yet, for the most part, selective universities' academic admission requirements benefit a particular kind of overachieving student at the expense of individuals who learn differently or are highly specialized in their skills and interests.

In an article analyzing "how to welcome and nurture the poets and painters of the future," for example, distinguished Harvard English Professor Helen Vendler reflects about the fact that "many future poets, novelists, and screenwriters are not likely to be straight-A students, either in high school or college. . . . Such unusual students may be, in the long run, the graduates of whom we will be most proud."[3] In her article, Professor Vendler poses difficult questions that all selective universities should ask themselves:

Do we have room for the reflective introvert as well as for the future leader? Will we enjoy the student who manages to do respectably but not brilliantly in all her subjects but one—but at that one surpasses all her companions? Can we see ourselves admitting such a student (which may entail not admitting someone else, who may have been a valedictorian)?

As these questions reveal, an outstanding student who does not fit the expected academic mold is usually at a disadvantage in selective universities' admissions process. Many times, however, universities would actually embrace this student's unique attributes despite an academic history that falls below expectations. For example, it may be the case that a student with no particular distinction in the humanities has come up with a new mathematical formula just at the time when a given college is seeking to strengthen its community of mathematicians. The challenge for these students is to convey their unique achievements and validate them through letters of recommendation from people familiar with their value. Just as important is explaining exactly how the student would take advantage of the university's resources and contribute to them in return.

Extracurricular Participation

For aspirants to a top university education, success in academics is necessary but by no means sufficient. Every year, thousands of students with excellent grades and test scores fail to gain acceptance to their preferred institutions. One reason for this is that the most selective universities seek not just outstanding students but also engaged youth with the experience, qualities, and passion to make a positive difference in society. College admission officers thus pay increasing attention to applicants' extracurricular history to evaluate what the student has accomplished outside of the classroom. Admissions officers believe that the quality (rather than the quantity) of the activities students choose to pursue in their free time can predict the student's potential contribution to the college community and the world at large.

In order to measure the quality of students' extracurricular activities, universities consider three main factors: genuine commitment, leadership, and impact. Students who are truly committed to their activities have remained involved through an extended period, taking advantage of opportunities to develop their participation and exploit their passions as much as possible. For example, a student who is truly excited about environmental conservation would join a school organization focused on the issue, take as many environmental science classes as possible, seek internships in the field, or attend conferences on the topic.

Selective universities also seek students who have accumulated leadership experience and excel in teamwork, oral communication, and strategic planning. Students can demonstrate this experience by participating in the boards of school or community organizations, by implementing their own independent projects, or even by taking care of younger siblings.

The value of these activities does not reside in their quantity or their perceived prestige. Colleges are suspicious of students who participate in so many activities simultaneously that it is impossible to enjoy or derive value from any of them, thus revealing that the student might just be trying to build a curriculum that impresses the colleges.

Colleges also question the value of dedicating endless hours to activities that do not produce self-development or do not elicit excitement in the student. Some people mistakenly compete in the accumulation of community service hours, regardless of their interest in the specific service activities they are performing. Other students just pursue the extracurriculars they think colleges prefer, underestimating the importance of their own interests.

Common beliefs about colleges' preference for certain extracurricular activities are often misleading. This particularly applies to varsity sports, which many students think are a virtual requirement to get into a prestigious college. Although it is true that some universities actively recruit student-athletes, admissions officers are mainly looking for students who have followed genuine personal interests. Dartmouth's Undergraduate Admissions website, for example, makes it clear that "there are no prescribed activities you should join that will get you into Dartmouth. Use your application to show us your passions and how you've been a contributing member of your community at home, school, and beyond."[4]

Indeed, it doesn't matter whether students' extracurricular involvement has taken place at school, the workplace, community organizations, or even the student's home. Regardless of the context and nature of the activity, what universities value are the student's commitment to their chosen endeavor and its social impact.

One reason varsity sports are particularly attractive to universities is the passion, engagement, and discipline they require. Relative to other extracurriculars, athletics demand a massive time commitment and exceptional teamwork skills. Colleges thus value athletics more for the qualities they reveal about an applicant, which non-athletes should demonstrate through other activities.

Since admissions officers review thousands of applications every year, they have become experts at determining whether applicants have truly pursued their passions in high school. When this has occurred, students describe their participation enthusiastically, and with great detail, in personal statements and personal interviews during the application process.

Character

Beyond academic and extracurricular potential, admissions officers place a strong emphasis on an applicant's moral qualities. Universities seek students who exhibit initiative, drive, compassion, maturity, adaptability, and perseverance. As chapter 8 of this book will explain in greater detail, students can demonstrate these qualities through letters of recommendation from teachers, personal statements, and interviews during the admissions process.

I did not truly understand the importance of universities' holistic admissions criteria until I arrived at Harvard. There I realized, almost immediately, that my most treasured source of learning and inspiration during my college journey would not be the courses, the faculty, the textbooks, or the student organizations.

Without a doubt, my peers were Harvard's greatest assets. I belonged in the most diverse class the University had ever attracted. For the third time in its history, women outnumbered men. We represented the widest range of economic backgrounds seen within a Harvard undergraduate class. Most of us were interested in the social sciences and humanities, but there was a strong inclination toward biological sciences, engineering, computer science, mathematics, and physical sciences, as well. We were coming from all around the world. My own roommates reflected our diverse ethnic composition: 19.2 percent Asian American, 9.3 percent African American, 8.8 Latino, and 1.2 Native American.[5]

Throughout my years at Harvard, my peers exposed me to mesmerizing intellectual and social experiences. They kept me up with long, late-night dining hall discussions that provided a good excuse to postpone homework until the early hours of the morning. With their help I polished my writing skills, became a better salsa dancer, and learned to cook exotic dishes like Irish butterscotch pudding. I traveled the world through their stories about growing up in Egypt, meditating in Asian Buddhist temples or sharing a household with eight siblings in suburban Baltimore. And I traveled the world with them, throughout Chile during time off from my internship at the government, or throughout European cities during breaks from my academic research in England and Spain.

My peers improved me, developed me, and challenged me. But most of all, they inspired me. I will always be grateful to the Harvard Admissions Office for bringing together such an extraordinary group of people through admissions policies that value human qualities as much as academic potential.

Some of you might be thinking that even if money is not directly considered in the admissions process, it surely has an impact. In the case of standardized testing, affluent students have easier access to expensive test preparation materials and courses. These students are also more likely to attend schools that offer a rigorous curriculum, including advanced courses such as IB and AP.

In the context of extracurricular activities, students from higher income families have an advantage as well. They can participate in high-priced summer enrichment programs, study abroad, or exploit a wider, richer network of contacts that supplies valuable opportunities. More affluent students can also pay the services of private college counselors and thus receive appropriate guidance to prepare for admission into top colleges. In contrast, low-income students are underserved by high school systems with an average ratio of one thousand students per counselor.

This reality is no reason for discouragement. The fact that wealthier students have an advantage in college preparation doesn't mean that students from low-income backgrounds cannot meet the academic and extracurricular admissions criteria, many times even more successfully. The key is to apply creativity and perseverance to exploit limited resources as much as possible, turning challenges into concrete opportunities for growth both within academics and extracurricular activities.

The next two chapters demonstrate how every talented low-income student can apply this strategy and develop the personal qualities necessary to be considered by top universities.

4

MEETING THE ACADEMIC ADMISSION REQUIREMENTS AT NO COST

It's often said that the way in which a person accomplishes something is at least as important as the accomplishment itself. Selective universities are fond of this philosophy. When reviewing applications for admission, they pay close attention not only to applicants' merits, but also, and especially, to *how* they have achieved these merits.

According to the website of Yale College Undergraduate Admissions:

> We are looking for students who will make the most of Yale and the most of their talents. Knowing how you've engaged in the resources and opportunities at your high school gives us an expectation of how you might engage the resources at Yale if admitted. In selecting future Yale students, President Brewster wrote, "I am inclined to believe that the person who gives every ounce to do something superbly has an advantage over the person whose capacities may be great but who seems to have no desire to stretch them to their limit." Within the context of each applicant's life and circumstances, we look for that desire and ability to stretch one's limits. [1]

Selective universities' appreciation for both the process and results associated with students' academic and extracurricular journeys means that admissions committees reward applicants who have demonstrated exceptional work ethic, ingenuity, and perseverance. In this respect, though it may seem counterintuitive, the presence of obstacles to become a competitive college applicant gives students an advantage: the opportunity to make exceptional efforts and show absolute commitment to the goal of attaining the finest college education.

High-achieving students with limited economic resources face unique potential obstacles to meet the academic admissions criteria described in the previous chapter. They may be unable to pay for the services of academic tutors. They may attend public schools that do not offer all the subjects students would like to take. They may find it difficult to get help preparing for standardized testing. These circumstances may seem discouraging, but they truly present extraordinary opportunities to stand out from the rest of the college applicant pool.

Instead of giving up because the available opportunities don't seem good enough to prepare for college, students should consider that schools are looking for people doing *the best they can* with the resources at hand. This chapter will outline specific strategies that low-income students may follow to build the most robust academic histories regardless of their economic status.

CHOOSING THE BEST POSSIBLE HIGH SCHOOL

Attending a good high school, whether it's public or private, provides the best chance to build a strong academic foundation for college. These are some characteristics that distinguish the kind of high school that best serves the needs of aspirants to top universities:

- Wide availability of subjects in core academic areas (mathematics, social studies, science, and English) as well as foreign languages
- Rigorous academic programs such as AP, IB, AICE, and IGCSE
- Presence of at least one college guidance counselor with a bachelor's degree
- High four-year college placement rates among recent graduates
- Admission of recent graduates to top colleges
- Awards for excellence won by students and faculty
- Availability of extracurricular opportunities

Most students face geographical constraints when choosing a public school, as they must attend one that is accessible from their homes, or one that falls within their assigned school zone. However, if there are no schools nearby that meet at least some of the characteristics described previously, students can also consider other opportunities. For example, they can attend magnet schools. These are institutions in the local public school system offering a rigorous academic curriculum with a focus on a particular field. A magnet school's population is not restricted to students from specific neighborhoods, and the schools usually apply a lottery-based admissions system.

Students may also consider attending some of the best private boarding schools in the country and around the world, which offer an excellent college preparatory curriculum. The prestigious Phillips Academy Andover, for example, provides as much financial aid as needed by a family to afford its high price. Many parochial schools are also accessible to low-income students through financial aid. For students who wish to explore other cultures, the United World Colleges (UWC) is another great option. These fourteen international institutions, which offer a large number of full scholarships, follow the IB curriculum and accept students based on their merit and potential to create a more peaceful society.

Given the multiple options available, students and their families should conduct very careful research before selecting a high school. Usually, individual schools have a website that offers ample information about the curriculum, staff and faculty, college placement, and extracurricular opportunities. It is also helpful to read the lists of best high schools published in local magazines and newspapers as well as national publications such as *Forbes* and *U.S. News and World Report*.

Some students fear that if they attend a very good high school that attracts a relatively large number of talented students, they will have a lower chance to stand out and thus get noticed by the most selective universities. This is a misconception. Universities do not limit the number of students they can accept from any given high school. On the contrary, they tend to accept a disproportionate number of applicants from the best high schools, known as "feeders."

Feeder high schools usually have established relationships with admissions offices at selective universities, and the latter trust the academic preparation of applicants coming from there. In fact, many colleges actually host interview events at select schools to make sure attractive candidates are not overlooked. Therefore, choosing a good high school not only increases a student's academic and extracurricular opportunities, but also improves admission chances at top universities.

PURSUING A RIGOROUS CURRICULUM

Regardless of the high school they attend, students with their hearts set on a top university must complete a rigorous curriculum that will demonstrate readiness for college-level academics. This entails taking as many high-level classes in the four core academic areas as possible.

Many high schools present challenges to the completion of this goal. A common one at schools with few resources is the lack of high-level course offerings in mathematics, science, social studies, and English. An institution, for example, may offer classes in algebra, geometry, and trigonometry, but not in statistics or calculus. Or it may offer AP U.S. History, but not AP World History or AP European History.

School policies regarding curriculum choices also affect a student's academic preparation for top colleges. Some schools restrict advanced classes to juniors or seniors. Others require students to take a number of vocational subjects such as physical education, arts, and computer literacy. Although these areas are important for students' overall development, they do limit students' capacity to get ahead in core fields. In both of these cases, students might feel compelled to forego the most rigorous curriculum they could pursue. Instead, they can ask for authorization from their schools to enhance the curriculum through additional resources such as online programs, summer school, or dual enrollment at local universities.

Tip: Students should consider joining forces to petition schools for specific subjects in core areas or foreign languages. In the past, students at schools around the country have successfully lobbied their principals for new classes in languages, for example, in an extra academic period.

When I was a freshman in high school with little knowledge of universities' academic expectations, I did not hesitate to pick the two most fun classes I found in the subject selection sheet: drama and typing. I certainly do not regret this decision; the performing arts helped me express myself more effectively, and typing was invaluable for fast note taking in college lectures. However, I could have easily acquired these skills outside of school, leaving more space for rigorous classes. From then on, I decided I would only take my school's advanced core classes, so I completed the required physical fitness and health credits during the summer session offered by my high school.

Most schools also limit the number of classes a student may take at the same time. When I was a junior, for example, I really wanted to take AP Art History as a seventh class, but the school did not allow me to take more than six courses during a single academic year. Therefore, I enrolled in the course through Florida Virtual School, a website that offers free online classes to students that reside in the state of Florida.

Schools may also impose strict requirements to access the most advanced classes. For example, they may require even the most gifted science students to take biology, chemistry, and physics at the honors level before they can study the same subjects at the AP level. Other students are discouraged from pursuing calculus because they are required to take algebra I, geometry, algebra II, and pre-calculus beforehand. Because many students take algebra I in ninth grade and often cannot take more than one math class every year, they think they will be unable to take math classes past pre-calculus.

Students with special talents in the math and sciences may follow a number of strategies to study these subjects at an advanced level before college. For example, they can pick a middle school that offers high school level subjects such as algebra I, geometry, earth science, and biology. That way, students enter their freshman year with a head start that allows them to take classes such as algebra II and chemistry from the very first semester. These students can also rely on dual-enrollment programs to accelerate their learning in these subjects.

As a high school sophomore, I had discovered that some of my peers were taking more advanced math classes such as algebra II, pre-calculus, and even calculus. They had been able to move ahead in the discipline because their middle schools had offered them high school level classes as early as seventh grade. I could not take advantage of this opportunity after arriving from Cuba so late into the last year of middle school. But I really wanted to study calculus, which I could only take after completing the algebra II and pre-calculus courses respectively assigned for my junior and senior years.

The only way I could catch up was completing one of the intermediate math classes during the summer vacations. Thus, I spent the summer after my sophomore year taking honors algebra II at Florida International University through Miami-Dade County's dual-enrollment program, which allows high school students in good academic standing to take courses at local universities at no cost. This experience was so rewarding that I returned to the dual-enrollment program the following summer to complete a Statistics class at Miami-Dade College (MDC). Coincidentally, one of my MDC classmates would begin her studies at Harvard at the same time as me.

Colleges appreciate students' initiative to take advantage of available academic opportunities such as online classes and dual-enrollment, demonstrating resourcefulness, self-discipline, time-management skills, and extraordinary focus on academic development. They also value students who use their spare time to learn something new outside of the high school curriculum.

Some students, for example, choose to study foreign languages independently, through online programs. Others teach themselves how to code. Nowadays, the wide availability of free distance learning classes (also known as Massive Open Online Courses or MOOCs) offered through platforms such as edX, Coursera, or Udacity makes it very easy to complement school learning.

Tip: edX has recently launched a collection of free courses specifically designed to prepare high school students for college-level academics. The courses, some of which are AP, range from mathematics to science, English, and history. Students can register for them at www.edx.org.

There are also opportunities to engage in academic research during the high school years, which can convey to colleges exceptional interest and knowledge in particular fields. Students may contact professors at local universities to ask whether it would be possible to shadow them or assist with research in the field, archives, or laboratories. It's also helpful to take courses in data analysis offered by some MOOCs.

Those who want to conduct research specifically in the sciences may also enter science competitions such as Intel Science Talent Search,

Intel International Science & Engineering Fair, Lemelson-MIT Inven-Teams, and the Siemens Competition. They may also apply to summer research programs such as the Research Science Institute (RSI), MIT MITES, the Summer Science Program (SSP), and the Program in Mathematics for Young Scientists (PROMYS). These programs are either free or offer financial aid to students who cannot pay the attendance costs.[2]

Among all forms of independent learning, colleges really value engagement during the summer breaks. Universities are attracted to self-driven students who seek every chance to develop skills or learn something new, and vacations provide ideal settings to test applicants' initiative. During the summer, students are on their own, and what they can accomplish depends largely on how they *choose* to organize their time and use the resources available.

There is a wide range of excellent summer programs for high school students, and many are hosted at the campuses of the nation's most selective colleges. Most of these programs are very pricey. Some, however, are free or offer significant scholarships to low-income students.

The MIT Office of Engineering Outreach Programs (OEOP), for example, offers three academic enrichment programs at no charge for high school seniors from across the country. The Asian American Journalists Association also hosts a free journalism training camp for high school students at a different college campus every summer. Princeton offers another intensive, free summer journalism program for high school students from low-income backgrounds. McCombs School of Business at the University of Texas at Austin is host to yet another free summer program in accounting and corporate leadership.

> Besides taking classes during my summers, I also caught up on reading, took a part-time job at a local gym, joined my high school's math team on a heavily subsidized trip to Hawaii to participate in a national math competition, and prepared for standardized tests. None of these activities required great wealth.

Still, some students face legitimate constraints that prevent them from undertaking an enriching summer activity. For example, some students might lack transportation to move around, or they might be forced to stay home to take care of a younger sibling. Students should explain such exceptional circumstances to colleges during the applica-

tion process, as admissions officers will consider students' limited resources and reward them even more for any initiative.

PREPARING FOR STANDARDIZED TESTING

As chapter 8 will explain in detail, most selective colleges require students to take standardized tests such as the SAT, ACT, and SAT Subject
Tests. Since these exams are complex and strictly timed, and because
they hold significant weight in college admissions decisions, the demand for preparation assistance has soared. This, in turn, has allowed
test prep companies to charge very high prices for prep courses and
materials, creating a gap between the training of students from high-
and low-income backgrounds.

However, there are a number of ways to prepare for the exam at no
cost. First, students should visit the websites of the organizations that
sponsor these exams, the ACT and the College Board, both of which
publish free guides and resources. The online learning company Khan
Academy offers full-length SAT practice tests and many math, reading,
and writing practice questions, along with videos that explain solutions
step-by-step. Recently, Khan Academy also launched a partnership with
the College Board to offer more sophisticated test prep tools such as
software diagnostics and state-of-the-art videos at no cost.

Expensive private test prep companies offer some free preparation
as well. The Princeton Review, for example, hosts "free events," a number of sessions around the country including practice exams, demon-
stration of test material and strategy workshops. Kaplan also hosts many
free online or in-person practice sessions. The single most important
component of successful test preparation, nonetheless, is consistent individual practice.

*Tip: Students can sign up for the Princeton Review's free events and
explore Kaplan's online or in-person practice sessions through the companies' respective official websites.*

When time came to study for standardized exams, my parents could
not afford private test prep courses or tutors, so I decided to study on

my own and not spend a cent in the process. Every Saturday morning, I would ask my mom or my dad to take me to the local library, where I would borrow the test prep guides from the shelves and devour them, not stopping until the sun had set and it was time to go home. When there was no more content left to read in the guides available at the library I moved to the local Barnes & Noble bookstore, which sold newer editions of the same guides and allowed students to browse them at the store. After consistent individual test preparation over the course of several months, I was able to score competitively on every exam.

Tip: It is very important to find a quiet space to focus on academics, including test preparation. Besides the local library or bookstore, students can consider their schools' own libraries and computer labs, the church or, in some cases, the college counselor's office.

In order to increase the chances of obtaining competitive scores in standardized tests, students should take these tests more than once. Low-income students might not consider this possibility given that each test charges a fee. However, before students register for the SAT, ACT, or SAT Subject Tests, they should determine whether they are eligible for registration fee waivers, which allow low-income students to take exams at no cost.

ACT offers fee waivers for a maximum of two exams, and the College Board offers four (up to two waivers for the SAT Subject Tests and up to two for the SAT). The waivers also allow students to send a number of free score reports to the colleges they select. Detailed information about requesting fee waivers and their coverage is available on the respective websites of the ACT and the College Board.

Tip: Notice that students must be in eleventh or twelfth grade to use an SAT fee waiver, or in ninth to twelfth grade to use a Subject Test fee waiver.

THE ROLE OF PARENTS

Students are the clear protagonists in the college application process. They are the ones who should ultimately decide whether to pursue post–high school studies and, if so, the kind of university environment and academic concentration they desire. In the same way, college aspirants are ultimately responsible for the academic and extracurricular choices they make in high school, and their results will largely depend on their individual efforts.

Nevertheless, the support of parents or caretakers along the way can make an extraordinary difference in students' preparation and confidence during this important period in their lives. In the context of high school academics, the help of parents is especially valuable. First and foremost, parents should help students identify and enroll in the best possible high school according to the criteria described earlier in this chapter. Once enrolled, students benefit from parents who understand the importance of a rigorous academic schedule and encourage students to stretch themselves to their limits.

Parental involvement in the school through regular interactions with teachers and administrators is also vital. For example, teachers appreciate parents' insights into personal circumstances that may pose challenges to students' academic performance. Parents should also approach college counselors and ask to remain informed about college visits, upcoming deadlines, and student scholarships.

Students from low-income families particularly benefit from strong support at home. When money is tight, students may feel pressured to work full-time to help their parents meet burdening costs. In these situations, parents should consider the long-term financial advantages of attending college, especially the most selective ones, and encourage students to devote appropriate time to rigorous academics, including homework. Students may still work part-time, or full-time during school breaks, but it is very difficult to combine a full workload with the most rigorous academic schedules.

Tip: The College Board offers a section especially designed for parents, including tips to apply for financial aid and webinars about steps that parents should take every year, starting in middle school, to help their children plan for college. Some colleges also have websites specifically for parents, including helpful handbooks on topics of interest, and even visiting events designed to inform the family as a whole.

I never would have succeeded in high school academics without my parents' support and encouragement. My parents were always at school when I needed them despite their inability to communicate fully with teachers and staff in English. As a freshman, for example, I begged my guidance counselor to enroll me in some honors classes. She hesitated; I had arrived from Cuba just a few months before and I still lacked strong English language skills. The only thing that worked was bringing my parents in so they could declare themselves responsible for the decision to enroll me in advanced courses.

Even though we lived in a very small apartment, where I had to share a room with my younger sister, my parents made every effort to grant me the privacy and tranquility to focus on my studies. They allowed me to take over the dining table every evening, covering it with so many books, folders and notebooks that there was barely any space left to have meals. They even helped with homework!

I relied on my mother's amazing mnemonic devices to ace exam components based on memorizing specific information. She sometimes got so creative with her mnemonics that I would break into laughter in the middle of a test, just remembering what she had come up with. Without my dad's tutoring, in turn, I would have struggled endlessly with physics assignments. They never questioned my decision to stay home during the weekends to study for an upcoming exam, or to carry a textbook with me during unavoidable outings.

With my parents' help, as the first semester of senior year drew to a close, I had already met the basic academic requirements to be considered a competitive candidate for top colleges. I had taken most of the advanced courses available at my high school, complementing them with other rigorous courses online and at local universities. I had maintained a perfect GPA. I was the first in the class rank. And I had obtained good scores on all standardized tests.

My academic journey had not benefited from expensive resources, but from the wide availability of advanced classes at my public high school, a wonderful group of dedicated teachers, my family's unconditional support and my own determination to do everything in my power to attain the best education possible.

5

HOW TO SUCCEED IN EXTRACURRICULARS WITHOUT SPENDING MONEY

Research shows that participating in extracurriculars leads to stronger academic performance, as demonstrated by higher grades, better standardized test scores, and fewer class absences. Active participants in extracurriculars also adjust better to the college setting, as they have a greater capacity to access support networks, interact more meaningfully with professors and adapt to diverse environments. (Notice, however, that these benefits decrease for students who participate in too many activities.)

Ever since I can remember, I have always been "involved." When my elementary school teachers asked for volunteers to participate in chorus or dance choreographies for school ceremonies, or if a teacher needed a student assistant, I always raised my hand. I became the president of student government during my first year in middle school, and would have to battle my parents to convince them that I did need to participate in such and such school camping trip or academic competition or vocational club.

Even after I moved to the United States and spent a while trying to understand how to become an active member of my new community, I quickly discovered things that attracted me outside of class. After all these years, if you asked me to pick just one element from my life that has shaped my general education, I would pick extracurricular activities.

There is no doubt that I owe my academic development to the lessons I received from excellent teachers all throughout my education. I could not have acquired strong critical thinking, reading comprehension and writing skills without taking many great classes and seminars from elementary school all the way through my master's program.

Yet, it was outside of the classroom, through extracurricular activities, that I developed leadership, communication skills, civic consciousness and the ability to work well with a diverse group of people. In retrospect, these skills have been at least as important as my formal academic training in both my personal and professional lives.

Many students feel they lack the time or the resources to participate in meaningful activities beyond schoolwork. Some, for example, might have to work when they are not in school. Colleges know that high school students sometimes combine studies with a part-time or, in some cases, even a full-time job. That's why, in the context of college applications, employment also counts as an extracurricular experience.

My mother's godfather, who has always been a mentor to my parents and me, recently shared the struggles he had to face in order to balance his academic and professional obligations during high school:

"As a low-income student, I had to work every weekday after school and on Saturdays throughout high school. I did so, not because I wanted to work, but because I had to work . . . I had to work so that we could pay the rent. Thus I did not have the luxury to participate in too many extracurriculars. I dreamed about playing left guard and wearing number 64 like Jerry Kramer of the Green Bay Packers but I had to stack books using the Dewey Decimal System while the other Jerry Kramer practiced and practiced so that we could win on Sunday!!!

My dad was making $1.25 per hour (not a typo) working six days a week selling shoes, and mom was at a toy factory making more or less the same amount. My $0.75 per hour (not a typo either) working in the reference department of the public library was much needed help to cover very basic costs. We did not have a penny but that was not my biggest lack . . . I did not have time to do anything but study and work . . . and walk five miles per day to get from the apartment to school to work and back again to the apartment."

Our inspiring mentor ended up graduating with a bachelor's degree in chemical engineering with honors, and launched an extremely successful corporate career that took him to over forty-nine countries.

Believe it or not, colleges greatly value students who have undergone job training. Many students take on low-wage part-time jobs at places such as fast food chains, coffee shops, or libraries, and don't think it is worth mentioning it in the college application. Yet, students with professional experience usually exhibit some of the qualities that are most attractive to colleges: responsibility, commitment, time management, and maturity. Therefore, students who combine rigorous high school studies with a job should not worry if they have no time left to devote to other activities. According to Harvard College Admissions:

> a student can gain a great deal from helping his or her family with babysitting or other household responsibilities or working in a restaurant to help with family or personal expenses. Such experiences are important "extracurricular" activities and can be detailed in the extracurricular section and discussed in essays. We realize that extracurricular and athletic opportunities are either unavailable or limited at many high schools. We also know that limited economic resources in many families can affect a student's chances for participation on the school teams, travel teams, or even prevent participation at all due to the costs of the equipment or the logistical requirements of some sports and activities. You should not feel that your chances for admission to college are hindered by the lack of extracurricular opportunities. Rather, our admissions committee will look at the various kinds of opportunities you have had in your lifetime and try to assess how well you have taken advantage of those opportunities.[1]

I was a sophomore in high school when I told my parents I wanted to buy my school's yearbook, which cost about one hundred dollars. My parents could not afford it, so I decided to work and earn the money I needed. Soon afterward I found employment at the cafeteria of a local gym, where my mother sometimes worked babysitting the children of the people who came to exercise. That was my first job.

Although my duties seemed simple—preparing protein shakes and fruit smoothies and serving them to sweaty customers—the experience required skills I had not developed in school. Managing a large volume of clients and following instructions from a strict supervisor, for example, were new challenges, and they taught me lessons I would not have learned otherwise.

I was so proud when I received my first check. I valued the feeling of working hard to accomplish a personal goal (in this case, my yearbook), saving my parents from an unnecessary financial burden. After that initial professional experience I realized that I could aspire to more skilled positions, and looked for jobs tutoring elementary and middle school students at their homes. I was fortunate that I didn't have to work full time to support my family, so I had time to combine these part-time jobs with non-professional extracurricular activities.

For some students, time is not an issue. Yet, they hesitate to seek extracurricular opportunities because of the perceived financial costs associated with these opportunities. In the same way that shining in academics does not require wealth (as explained in the previous chapter), students from low-income families can pursue extracurriculars at little or no cost during both academic and vacation periods. Below are some tips to accomplish a rewarding and affordable extracurricular journey throughout the high school years.

FIND WHAT YOU LOVE

The key to successful participation in extracurriculars is to engage in what truly drives you, whatever that is. When we enjoy a pastime, we are most likely to give it our all and to exploit all the opportunities for growth that it offers. Students should take advantage of this rare flexibility in the high school experience, so dominated by strict academic requirements. By following genuine interests, students will be more likely to stand out from other college applicants.

Many people believe that colleges have a preference for certain activities such as varsity sports, orchestra, or honor societies, and so they end up presenting very similar extracurricular histories in their applications. Since people naturally exhibit different interests, staying true to them is the best way to ensure our applications reflect our uniqueness.

One proof that selective colleges are open to a wide range of interests is the variety of student-run extracurricular organizations on campus. Here is just a sample from Harvard College: Anime Society, Undergraduate Beekeepers, Culinary Society, Robotics Club, and Wine Society. Some of Princeton's undergraduate clubs are 3D Printing, Beach Volleyball Club, Billiards Club, Bread Houses Network Club, and Global Poker Strategic Thinking Society. Duke has the Coalition Against Wrongful Convictions, the Bass Fishing Team, the Homebrewing Club, and the Swing Dance Club. Students at the nation's most selective universities are open to incredibly specific and varied interests.

EXPLORE OPPORTUNITIES AT SCHOOL

Once students have identified their interests, they should investigate possible spaces to pursue them in their high schools. Most schools offer a number of clubs that students can join at no cost, with meetings usually taking place in the afternoon after classes end. If the school website does not publish information about clubs available, teachers, counselors, and administrators can inform students of extracurricular offerings.

Participating in high school clubs is the easiest way to get involved. Since club activities normally happen on school grounds, students don't have to travel any distance or incur in transportation costs in order to participate. The presence of teachers and classmates in these clubs also facilitates participation, as there are more opportunities for collaboration. At the same time, many schools are willing to let students develop their own clubs or projects with school resources. In these cases, students can easily recruit membership from the school's student population.

Three particular extracurricular categories are usually present in high schools across the nation: sports teams, community service clubs, and academic honor societies. Student-athletes can take advantage of school sports to compete at the district, state, and national levels without having to pay for expensive private sports clubs or hire a personal coach or trainer. However, some private coaches are willing to accept low-income students with extraordinary talents in sports, at no cost, if they think the student will contribute significant value to the team.

Through community service clubs, students can not only devote themselves to causes they may care about deeply such as childcare, environmental sustainability, senior citizens' wellbeing, literacy, or cultural integration, to name a few. Service clubs also allow students to become active members in their communities and create valuable relationships with a wide range of people, many times beyond the local neighborhood. Two particular service organizations, Key Club and Interact, are the respective school chapters of the Kiwanis and Rotary international organizations. This means that Key Club and Interact members have exposure to a powerful network of equally service-oriented individuals from all around the world.

Finally, honor societies are organizations that select members based on academic excellence. High schools usually have chapters of national honor societies such as Mu Alpha Theta (the Mathematics Honor Society), the Science Honor Society, the English Honor Society, and a variety of foreign language honor societies. These clubs have broad missions and allow students to conduct a wide range of activities in the school and the surrounding community.

Some students might not be attracted to any of the clubs established at their high school. In this case, they may consider a few options. First, if students have a very specific activity in mind, they can petition their schools to launch a new organization to pursue it, which can be done at no cost. To finance particular activities within the new club, students can organize fundraising events with the help of members and the school at large.

A school, however, might limit the number of student organizations or discourage students from starting their own. If that's the case, students can take advantage of umbrella organizations such as the honor societies, which often allow members, especially those on the executive board, to develop individual initiatives. Students can also look beyond the school to pursue their unique interests.

EXPLORE OPPORTUNITIES OUTSIDE OF SCHOOL

The most competitive college applicants exhibit a strong sense of awareness about their communities, however they may define them. It may be their local neighborhood. It may be their ethnic group. It may even be the world at large. Regardless of the nature of the community, these students are deeply engaged in it and devise creative ways to apply its resources to make a positive difference. As the website of Columbia's Undergraduate Admissions explains, these students are more likely to take "the greatest advantage of the [college] experience and offer something meaningful in return."[2]

It is not necessary to belong to a wealthy community to enjoy extra-curricular experiences outside of school. Communities with scarce resources actually offer more opportunities for individual engagement and impact through service-oriented activities.

Many students seek volunteering opportunities at local organizations such as the church, nursing homes, hospitals, public schools, and non-profits in a variety of areas such as health, education, and social welfare. Students can provide very valuable help to these organizations; for example, they can offer academic tutoring through after-school programs, organize fundraising events for local nonprofits, or entertain hospital patients or nursing home residents.

Most communities also offer spaces to pursue very specific interests. With the help of the Internet, students can usually find institutions or other people who share unique passions or missions, and even collaborate virtually. There are online communities of writers, programmers, and pretty much anything. And if there isn't one that caters to a student's extremely specific interest, there are many free tools to create a blog or forum and build your own. The Internet also offers the opportunity to work from the distance, performing a wide range of jobs such as editing, coding, or researching.

SCALING YOUR INITIATIVE

Selective universities pay attention not only to the kind of activities students pursue, but also to the *quality* of these activities. Therefore, college aspirants should strive to scale their projects inside and outside of school as much as possible, maximizing leadership and impact. This can also be done at no cost to the student, and usually involves three main aspects: teamwork, fundraising, and publicity.

It is very difficult to organize large-scale initiatives without the help of others, especially when the leader is a busy high school student with a full load of rigorous academics. The easiest way to recruit help is through the existing membership of a school club. Leaders can also partner with similar clubs at other schools and enlist the help of their members as well. Outside of schools, students can reach out to relatives' friends and colleagues. The Internet also offers crowdsourcing platforms, which are sites that facilitate a wide range of contributions from a large group of people at a distance.

Many times, large-scale projects require expenses that low-income students cannot afford. Fortunately, there are various ways to obtain financial help. First, students can apply for a number of grants specifically to implement a project. The application for these scholarships normally requires a detailed project proposal outlining the costs, timeline, and impact of the project. Some examples of national grants are the Do Something Awards, Miami Dolphins and NFL Junior Community Quarterback Award, and the Lemelson-MIT InvenTeams. Given the variety of grants, students should conduct an online search to find those that apply to their specific initiatives.

Another funding resource is a kind of crowdsourcing called crowdfunding, a type of online platform that allows individuals or organizations to collect funds from Internet users via donations. Some of the most popular crowdfunding sites are www.gofundme.com, www.kickstarter.com, and www.indiegogo.com.

Tip: Low-income high school students living in New York, Los Angeles, or the San Francisco Bay Area can apply to participate in the programs of an organization called Wishbone, a not-for-profit fundraising platform that identifies students who can't afford to pursue their passions and funds their participation in an enriching summer program. Learn more at www.wishbone.org.

In order to spread awareness about initiatives, recruit funds and supporters, or simply meet other people who share the same interests, students can pursue a number of publicity strategies. The Internet offers a wide range of free marketing spaces, starting with social media such as Facebook, Instagram, and Twitter. However, students can also look into attending conferences, summer programs, and competitions about their particular topic of interest. A student's high school can also help by publishing information on its official website, newsletter, or social media pages.

As a high school student, my limited resources did not stop me from pursuing my passions. The fact that most students at my school were Hispanic and many had recently moved to the United States from their native countries had opened my eyes to the extraordinary difficulties faced by immigrant families like mine when preparing their children for high-quality university education. Most parents did not understand the college application process, and lacked sufficient English language skills to read college admissions websites or communicate with college representatives. My parents' support had always been essential for my academic development and college planning, so I understood the gravity of the situation and sought to do something about it.

I started by enlisting the help of some friends to produce a document that contained vital information in Spanish regarding college planning. My friends and I then distributed this document among parents during the school's open house, and visited every class to deliver short presentations on the subject. The project escalated as we improved the quality of the document, turned it into a newsletter and built a website. Around the same time, I heard from my school's Key Club coordinator that ACT was looking to hire Hispanic high school students to write an online diary about their college planning experiences. I immediately expressed interest and became the first ACT blogger to produce articles in both English and Spanish, focusing on increasing college awareness among Hispanic families.

Beyond my activities in college awareness, I was also very involved in student organizations at school. Given my interest in math I joined the Mu Alpha Theta Mathematics Honor Society as early as tenth grade. Every month, our group would participate in competitions at different schools in the state, which allowed me to meet many talented students and explore a bunch of neighboring towns. My wonderful experiences as a member of the club motivated me to join the board as historian in eleventh grade, and as president in twelfth grade.

I also sought every space my school offered to pursue my passion for writing and literature. Ms. Cabrera, the inspiring English teacher who organized field trips to dreamy Renaissance festivals, constantly motivated us to submit our work to contests such as the Scholastic Art and Writing Awards.

I actively participated in Key Club, as well, the oldest and largest service program for high school students. I first discovered this club during the second semester of my freshman year. One afternoon, I noticed a particularly excited crowd in the school's backyard. One girl was standing on a lunch table, addressing a large group of enthusiastic listeners. I got close and realized she was describing a series of events that would take place very soon. Horse riding therapy sessions for children with disabilities. Neighborhood feasts and toy sales for low-income families. Visits to local nursing homes to entertain residents. Everyone seemed genuinely engaged with the news, and I was instantly convinced that I wanted to become part of this special group. I joined right away. The following year, I was vice president. And by the time junior year arrived, I was the president.

So it was that despite my limited resources I had a very rich academic and extracurricular high school experience. This was possible largely because my school offered a large variety of advanced courses and multiple student organizations, and because a number of teachers generously volunteered to support students' extracurricular activities. Ultimately, however, what made the difference in my preparation to become a competitive applicant to top colleges was my determination to take advantage of all available resources and prioritize my learning and integral development above everything else.

This ensured that when time came to fill out the college applications, I was ready. Or so I thought.

6

FINDING ACCESSIBLE COLLEGE COUNSELORS

The Expert and the Role Model

Even the most talented students benefit from guidance during the college application process. They might have perfect grades and the most rigorous academic schedules. They might have an outstanding extracurricular record. They might be extremely motivated, lead in their communities, and exhibit unique qualities and life experiences. And yet, the advice from knowledgeable and caring individuals might make the difference in these students' transition to the nation's most selective undergraduate programs.

In order to become a competitive college applicant, it is not sufficient to accumulate impressive academic and extracurricular histories. Students must also apply to colleges *strategically* to highlight their unique strengths and maximize their chances of admission.

As the next two chapters will explain in detail, this strategy requires careful consideration of the list of colleges to which students should apply, the number of applications that should be submitted, the content of the required application essays, the teachers who will provide recommendation letters, the benefits of an early versus regular round application, and many other issues. In order to tackle each of them effectively, students would do well to seek the advice of college counselors—the people with substantial experience coaching students on the application procedures, the expectations of specific colleges and the unique ways in which individual students can enhance their application.

When one thinks about college counseling, two figures usually come to mind: the high school official appointed to help students navigate the college application process and the private counselor who offers college guidance outside of the school system. In theory, both figures represent what I call the "expert," a professional who provides the information and strategy to ensure that students maximize their chances of admission at the best possible undergraduate institutions.

Besides experts, there is a second source of college advice that is at least as important: the role model. In the context of college admissions, role models are personal mentors who advise applicants based on their own experiences preparing for college. Unlike experts, who may not have graduated from institutions in which students are interested, role models have the unique power to transmit energy and inspiration through real-life examples of success. These ingredients are crucial to motivate students who fear they will be unable to make it into college, especially the most selective schools.

Contrary to what many people think, securing the help of an expert and role model during the college application period does not necessarily involve great economic resources. All it requires is motivation and knowledge about a few strategies and resources, outlined in this chapter.

FINDING A COLLEGE COUNSELING EXPERT

High school is the first place where students should look for expert college guidance. Normally, every school hires at least one counselor who is responsible for college placement, one of the most important measures of a school's effectiveness and prestige. Students should identify and establish rapport with the counselor even before senior year, as they will benefit from early orientation regarding course selection, extracurricular participation, standardized testing, and general enrichment opportunities.

Once students enter the college application period, they should seek the advice of their counselor to decide target colleges, craft an appropriate application timeline, prepare an application that enhances their strengths, and explore financial aid options. Because some colleges require (and most welcome) a letter of reference from applicants' school counselors, students benefit from building fruitful, long-term relationships with this staff, enabling the letters to reflect familiarity with students' personal and academic achievements.

Given the complexity of the college application process, the guidance of a professional in the field can make a significant difference in the submission of a strong application. This help is especially valuable if students have grown up with little exposure to the application process (if, for example, they are the first in their families to attend college).

Sadly, research shows that many counselors across the nation are unable to provide the one-on-one expert advice students require to apply successfully to an appropriate range of colleges. On the one hand, it is common to have hundreds of students assigned to a single college counselor, which makes it difficult for the counselor to provide individualized attention unless the student stands out and takes the initiative to seek counseling early. A recent study by the U.S. Department of Education even finds that one in five high schools in the nation lacks a school counselor.[1]

On the other hand, some counselors are not adequately trained to provide these specialized services. It has also been shown that some of them can even directly hurt applicants' admissions chances at the nation's most selective institutions when, for example, they recommend capable students *not* to take as many higher-level courses as would be desirable. Other counselors promote nonselective institutions excessively, luring talented low-income students with the promise of lower tuition rates and less selectivity.

Some counselors' general lack of expertise about the admissions and financial aid processes at the top colleges ultimately drives away very strong candidates from the extraordinary opportunities these colleges offer. This reality has motivated many families to seek college counseling from independent experts. Yet, most private counselors charge very high fees in exchange for their services, limiting their benefits to students in the middle and upper-income sectors.

Tip: As soon as they enroll in high school, students should approach the official in charge of college counseling and start a conversation about college plans. It is worthwhile to write the counselor an introductory e-

CHAPTER 6

52

mail, explaining academic and extracurricular interests as well as preliminary thoughts about the kind of higher education they are seeking.

Students with limited economic resources have other alternatives to receive expert college guidance:

1. Apply to a college prep program. Many programs throughout the country offer individualized college guidance to low-income students *at no cost*, with the added benefit of providing a network of like-minded peers with similar backgrounds and motivation for college. The programs are incredibly varied. Whereas some take place after school or during the summer, others last for years, coaching students through college as well. Some programs even offer their own scholarships to help participants meet the costs of their degrees, provide free preparation for the SAT and ACT and facilitate visits to college campuses. Most importantly, these programs are well regarded at the most selective institutions, some of which are direct partners and commit to accept at least some of the program participants.

The following are some examples of the national programs that low-income students in particular should consider:

- Sponsors for Educational Opportunities SEO Scholars
- QuestBridge
- Posse Foundation
- Simon Scholars
- Juma Ventures
- College Track
- The College Place

The National College Access Directory offers information about many more programs that operate within specific geographical areas.

Tip: College prep programs usually have very early application deadlines, sometimes during a student's second or third year of high school. Students should therefore check the programs' respective websites as early as freshman year to keep in mind tentative application dates and set reminders to return to the websites for updated information.

2. Seek help from a counselor from another school. Even though most high school counselors are overburdened, some are surprisingly willing to "adopt" star students from other schools who are underserved by their own counselors. Students should proactively approach friends, relatives, and acquaintances who may be familiar with an effective counselor, and ask these references to make an introduction. It is possible that even if students find such counselor, he or she may not have the time to provide on-one-one guidance over a long period. Yet, the counselor could do a number of valuable things that require little time such as introducing the student to potential role models, recommending a list of target colleges, and adding students as recipients of notifications about scholarships, application deadlines, and other relevant information.

3. Contact target colleges' admissions offices. Many students don't realize that admissions offices do not merely evaluate college applications. A big part of their responsibilities is to provide guidance to prospective students in many different ways. For example, admissions officers usually deliver open information sessions at high schools and other venues across the country, an excellent opportunity for one-on-one meetings. Admissions offices also host info sessions and campus tours at the actual colleges. Through these offices' websites, students can find helpful tips about the application to the particular school, sign up to receive notifications from the college, and even read blogs written by current students about their academic and social experiences.

Most selective colleges employ a number of students at the admissions offices to provide advice to applicants by e-mail and phone. Applicants should take advantage of this unique opportunity to get a personal perspective about life on a given college campus, as well as to request advice on the application from someone that went through the same process recently and successfully.

At some colleges, admissions officers are also available to respond to e-mails from prospective students. However, students should be careful not to abuse this opportunity (and hurt their chances of admission) by sending too many communications or asking for information easily found on the college's official website. Even

Dartmouth's admissions website, which states they "won't hold it against you if you ask us a really basic question," tells you right after that "BEFORE YOU CONTACT US: Use the website's search feature [and] check out our FAQs."[2] A good rule of thumb is to make these communications personal and relevant to the college application process, and to limit the number of interactions.

When I was in high school, I sent admissions officers at some of my target colleges one or two e-mails to confirm that my twelfth-grade academic schedule would be considered rigorous. And whenever I met admissions officers at college information sessions hosted in my hometown, I would always introduce myself, request their business card and follow up with additional questions by e-mail. Most colleges keep a record of these interactions with prospective students and take into the account the sustained interest when making an admissions decision.

Tip: Students should keep in mind that admissions officers will take advantage of any preliminary communication to evaluate a prospective applicant. Students should strive to present themselves professionally, selecting an e-mail address that conveys their maturity. E-mail addresses that combine a person's first and last name are advisable. Students should avoid addresses that contain nicknames or words that may be considered offensive. Every e-mail communication, moreover, should include a proper subject line, salutation, body paragraphs, and signature, avoiding errors in spelling and grammar.

The Internet also offers vast information about general college admissions, and most of it can be accessed for free. As is usually the case with the Internet, however, the trick is to find a source that offers complete, reliable, relevant, and updated information. Besides the official website of the College Board, students will find very helpful content at www.khanacademy.org/college-admissions, the college admissions series recently launched by the online distance learning provider Khan Academy. Through this page students can access a series of videos—some featuring accounts by real college students—about many important topics in the college application process.

FINDING A ROLE MODEL

As is the case with college counselors, high schools are the first stop in the search for a role model. In late fall and early spring, freshmen, sophomores, and juniors should approach the seniors admitted to the same colleges they are considering and request advice regarding preparation for postsecondary studies.

Having mentors from one's own high school is highly beneficial. They can provide information about how to maximize local resources, both in the school and community. They can recommend specific classes from the school curriculum, particularly enriching student organizations and helpful counselors. They can also lend test preparation materials and even invite students to their future college campus. The exact help a role model provides varies, and deeper relationships will likely depend on the personal chemistry between mentors and students. But the nature of the interaction will invariably yield benefits to both.

In the United States, there are also more structured mentorship programs at no cost to students. Many of these organizations recruit volunteers from college or the workforce and match them with college aspirants from specific high schools or geographic regions, mostly in low-income communities. The programs also offer a wide range of additional benefits such as leadership development, career orientation, and recreation opportunities. These are just some of the mentorship programs available:

- Strive for College
- MENTOR: The National Mentoring Partnership
- iMentor
- College Advising Corps (CAC)
- College Mentoring for Access and Persistence (College MAP)

MY ESSENTIAL COLLEGE COUNSELORS

In the spring of my junior year, the brilliant son of family friends was accepted to many selective colleges and decided to attend Harvard. As soon as my parents heard this news, they pressed me to meet with him and seek his guidance. I was a little intimidated by the idea. I was not convinced that I too could aspire to the kind of universities that had just admitted him, and didn't want to waste his time.

But my parents insisted, and just a few days later I was already on my way to the meeting where the seeds of a wonderful friendship were planted over iced coffee—surely a sign that the universe was bringing together two of its most "caffeinated" spirits. In the months that followed, David would become my guide through the college application process. And through our years together at Harvard and beyond, he would always stand by my side as the older brother I never had.

The reassuring and inspiring presence of a true mentor made an extraordinary difference as I navigated the complex applications to multiple universities. Throughout David's last semester of high school, when he was juggling a full load of AP classes, extracurricular leadership positions, and a part-time job delivering newspapers, he would still make time to drive for over an hour to meet me at my house and train me for the math section of the SAT, or help me brainstorm college essay topics.

Thanks to David, I was also able to visit Harvard for the first time. In the fall semester of my senior year, I spent two nights sleeping on a couch in the living room of the freshman dorm David shared with three roommates. It was an unforgettable experience. I saw the snow for the first time in my life, partied in upper-class houses, and attended academic lectures. I even accompanied David to his rehearsal for an upcoming performance with the same salsa dance team I would be joining less than a year later.

David's greatest gift, however, was Ms. Collins, a math teacher for over thirty years who now worked as a guidance counselor at David's high school. She was the one who had called him into her office two years earlier upon seeing his stellar grades, to ask him whether he was aware he had the potential to get into the top universities. This episode was emblematic of her star-seeking nature. Her own daughter had attended Harvard, and Ms. Collins had guided countless other students onto formidable academic paths at the nation's most selective colleges. Her magic was to distinguish promise in her students, to believe in them, and to make them believe in themselves.

It was thus no surprise that David's first instruction after our meeting was to contact Ms. Collins right away. I still keep that first e-mail I sent to her just a few days later, confiding all my hopes to her expert eyes. Her response came without delay, and left me with awe:

Dear Maria:

I am highly impressed with what you are doing and what you have done. You are definitely HARVARD MATERIAL.

Ms. Collins' uplifting arrival into my life changed it forever. She instilled in me the courage to trust and seize my chances of getting into any university. She shared her infinite wisdom about college application strategies. She made herself available, at all times, always with a smile on her face and enthusiasm in her voice. And she did not ask for anything in return.

From the moment I met Ms. Collins, I certainly felt that my college aspirations largely hung from her thread. Even though I had built an academic and extracurricular resume that most colleges would have considered competitive, I felt that my ignorance about many aspects of the application process could still jeopardize my admission results. For example, which colleges should I consider? Should I submit both my SAT and ACT score reports or just one of them? To how many colleges should I apply? Should I submit Early Action or Early Decision applications? If so, to which colleges? Which topics would be strategic for my personal statements?

In my school, despite their best efforts, the guidance counselors lacked the resources to provide effective, individualized attention to the more than one thousand students in our graduating class. I appreciated my counselors' general support and encouragement, as well as their notifications about particular scholarships or their initiative to host an annual college talk, to which they would invite recent graduates who were enjoying successful undergraduate experiences. But when time came to seek one-on-one counseling on the college application process, the best my fellow seniors and I could do was turn to experts like Ms. Collins or role models like David.

With their help, now I was truly ready to apply.

7

HOW TO CHOOSE TARGET COLLEGES IN THREE STEPS

With over four thousand colleges in the United States, deciding where to apply is one of the most difficult decisions high school students will ever have to make. Sometimes it's not even clear where the search should begin, as there is no complete registry of colleges that includes all the information that students should consider before they make their selection. Such information is not straightforward, either. According to their personal circumstances, different students will assign different value to the many aspects in which universities differ. The task of sorting through so many institutions may seem so daunting that students might choose to apply only to the colleges with which they are familiar.

Research shows that high-achieving students from low-income families do not generally pursue the overarching goal of the college application process, which is getting into the best possible schools. Unlike many talented students from wealthy backgrounds, the majority of lower income students do not apply to colleges that offer a rigorous curriculum that matches their academic training, even when they are likely to be admitted. Regardless of their talents, low-income students apply mostly to local community colleges or four-year institutions with few resources and low graduation rates. Many low-income high-achievers, in fact, apply only to nonselective colleges.[1]

College counselors would never advise this application behavior. They know that even though it is practically impossible to guarantee a student's admission into specific universities, there is a strategy to maximize the chances of admission into colleges that best serve students' academic, professional, and personal interests. This strategy involves three main elements: 1) determining an adequate number of applications, 2) considering colleges with a wide range of admissions probabilities, and 3) identifying the college characteristics of critical importance to the individual student.

THE RIGHT NUMBER OF TARGET COLLEGES

Although there isn't a "right" number of college applications, some factors can help students figure out the right number *for them*, given their specific circumstances. This magical number largely depends on the amount of time, effort, and money students are willing to put into the process.

A general rule of thumb is to submit high-quality applications to a small number of universities than apply carelessly to many. Crafting an effective college application is a complex process that requires dedication over a period of several months. Some students underestimate the difficulty of the application period because they believe it basically entails filling out a simple form, sending transcripts and letters of recommendation, and writing a short essay. As the next chapter will explain, this could not be further from the truth.

Selective colleges, in particular, usually require additional essays and letters of recommendation, as well as personal interviews and scores from specific standardized tests. On top of this, colleges expect accurate applications that reflect a candidate's qualities truthfully. Aspirants to top universities should thus factor in extra time to revise the application multiple times. This means students should only submit as many applications as they can realistically complete with the expected quality and without neglecting their parallel obligations in their personal and academic lives.

Another factor to consider when applying to college is the cost of each application. Most colleges in the United States require students to pay an application fee that can range from thirty to almost one hundred dollars. Even though low-income students may qualify for fee waivers, these are usually limited. College counselors therefore estimate that applying to more than thirteen universities would impose an unnecessary and unmanageable burden to students both financially and logistically.

At the same time, given the great likelihood of rejection at the most selective colleges, students should apply to a number of universities that is large enough to generate a few final choices to pick from. It is advised that students do not apply to fewer than eight or nine universities if the majority of the target institutions are at least somewhat selective.

Tip: High school students should pick between eight and thirteen target colleges.

LIKELIHOOD OF ADMISSION

Strategically, high-achieving students aspiring to enter the nation's top colleges should apply to institutions with a wide range of likelihood of admission. In the college admissions lingo, "reach" universities are those that are most difficult for a student to get into. "Peer" or "match" colleges are those where admission is likely but not guaranteed. Finally, institutions where students are extremely likely to get in are called "safety." Counselors recommend that high-achieving students apply to three to five reach, three to five peer, and at least two safety institutions to maximize the chances of admission.

Normally, a university is considered reach if its admissions rate is extremely low and/or the applicant's GPA and standardized test scores are significantly below the median of current students, peer if the applicant's GPA and test scores are on par with the median, and safety when current students have median GPAs and test scores significantly below the applicant's.

Tip: To find out the median standardized test scores and other characteristics of current students at specific universities, visit the institutions' individual admissions websites and look for sections called "admissions statistics," "class profile," or "admitted students profile." This information sometimes appears under the "counselors" section.

62

CHAPTER 7

A university's selectivity is not to be confused with universities' admissions rates, which simply measure the percentage of applicants admitted to the university. In contrast, selectivity refers to how difficult it is for a *specific student* to get into that university. The difference between these two concepts is subtle, but it is an important one. While admissions rates are *objective*, selectivity is *subjective*. In other words, selectivity depends on how the applicant compares to the kinds of students usually admitted to the university. For example, a student with a perfect GPA and standardized test scores and many achievements outside of the classroom might consider the top state school a safety even if this school's admissions criteria are still selective. Another student who became motivated later in high school and accumulated various grades below the B level might deem the same state school a reach.

Besides the students' grades and test scores, other qualitative factors can also be taken into account to predict a student's likelihood of admission into specific universities. The following three, for example, are particularly strong indicators: legacy, athletic value, and relationship with high school.

An applicant enjoys "legacy status" at particular universities when any relatives have attended the same institution. Universities, especially selective ones, have traditionally given preference to so-called legacies among applicants with similar academic and extracurricular credentials. Students should thus ensure they mention in the application the names of any graduates within the family.

Athletes are more likely to be admitted to specific universities as well if these institutions place special value on the student's sport. If a student has exhibited exceptional athletic abilities in high school, and has serious intentions of playing sports at a competitive level in college, he or she should approach the high school's coach early on and ask for recommendations about schools that specialize in the student's sport of choice as well as general eligibility requirements.

Serious athletes should also communicate directly with college coaches no later than tenth grade. It is worth remembering that playing a sport in high school will be valued by colleges as a terrific extracurricular activity even if the student is not recruited as an athlete to play in the college's teams.

Tip: The National Collegiate Athletic Association (NCAA), the National Association of Intercollegiate Athletics (NAIA), and the National Junior College Athletic Association (NJCAA) offer resources for student-athletes' preparation for college. Prospective college athletes should consider applying to be certified as an initial qualifier through the NCAA Division I Certification Clearinghouse. Information about this process is available on the NCAA website.

A university's strong relationship with a high school—which occurs when the school has a history of sending strong candidates to the university—may also give applicants an extra edge in the admissions process. Before compiling a list of target colleges, students should thus approach the college counselor and general administration and ask if there are any particular universities that consistently accept at least a few students from their high school.

Finding the colleges where applicants have a high chance of getting in is just one part of the college search. For every talented high school student, there are generally many more schools that would offer an admission letter than those he would actually like to attend. In order to choose the select number of institutions that will make it into the final target list, students should identify what I call critical characteristics—the necessary conditions that must be met by a university for students to feel that they would enjoy studying *and* living within its gates.

CRITICAL CHARACTERISTICS

Choosing target colleges feels a little bit like dating. Usually, before one even sets eye on a specific person, there is intense awareness of the characteristics we are looking for in our ideal romantic partner. And we might give different weight to each characteristic. For example, someone might place a high value on characteristics like religious affiliation or a fun personality, but not so much on dancing skills.

Assessing colleges is no different. Students must explore their own tastes very carefully and determine these tastes' relative weight before they select and pursue their targets. The following are general areas that students should consider as they think about their ideal higher education experience:

Academics

- Curriculum. Most top colleges in the United States offer a "liberal arts education," a broad curriculum that requires students to specialize in one area but also become well versed in a wide range of academic disciplines such as history, philosophy, natural sciences, physical sciences, mathematics, and literature. The liberal arts model has been praised for teaching students the creative, communication, and analytical skills that enable them to succeed in any professional path.

  Instead of liberal arts, other top universities in the United States (for example, many technology institutes) offer a pre-professional curriculum, which emphasizes training for specific careers such as engineering, business and law. A third group of universities, such as MIT and Penn, integrate aspects of both the liberal arts and pre-professional curricula into their unique instructional models. Students should pay close attention to a university's curriculum, as it normally influences course requirements and the diversity of academic majors available.

- Academic concentrations. Some students have a very clear idea about the majors and/or minors they would like to pursue in college. If so, they should pick target colleges that offer them. Other students are not set on specific disciplines, but are inclined toward a general academic area such as the natural sciences. In this case, students should consider colleges that offer multiple majors in the area of interest.

  For students completely undecided about their academic concentrations, colleges that offer and excel in a wide range of disciplines are usually the best choice. Applicants should also pay close attention to the extent to which a college allows students to explore different disciplines before selecting a major, as well as the requirements to change from one academic concentration to another.

Tip: About 50 to 80 percent of students change their majors at least once during the college period. It is thus better to apply to colleges that offer a wide range of options than to choose a school based on the strength of a single academic program.

- Course offerings. Perhaps more important than academic concentrations are the specific courses offered within each major or minor. Even majors with the same name can differ greatly across universities in terms of requirements, specialization, and number of courses available.
- Faculty. The caliber and volume of faculty members add extraordinary value to the academic experience. Students should consider whether there are specific professors they would like to learn from and possibly even assist with research. At the same time, they should consider the percentage of faculty members who hold PhDs, the percentage of courses at the university taught by professors (as opposed to graduate students) and the student-to-faculty ratio. Normally, smaller ratios indicate smaller class sizes and more opportunities to work closely with professors.
- Classmates. In the same way that high-achieving students benefit from outstanding faculty, a group of accomplished peers will provide a greater academic experience. Fellow high-achievers are more likely to engage in stimulating debates, contribute to the learning of new material, and cultivate an intellectual and innovative environment. For indicators of a university's collective student accomplishment, it is useful to look at the academic admissions criteria and any mention of academic recognition among current students.
- Academic advising. College students, especially freshmen and sophomores, benefit from the guidance of experts when making decisions regarding their studies. The best advisers are usually academics with many years of experience working at the university level. Applicants should pay attention not only to the kinds of advisers available, but also to the number of students each adviser is assigned as well as the number of times a student is able to meet with the adviser each semester. More productive relationships arise when meetings between advisers and students are frequent, and when only a few students are assigned to each adviser.
- Academic research. Many students aspire to conduct their own investigations in a particular field, and some institutions offer this opportunity at the college level. Research opportunities vary from college to college. At some institutions, students conduct research as part of the curriculum in specific courses, or they can assist a professor with ongoing research. Some universities provide facilities such as labora-

tories for research in the sciences, and others have a wide range of research positions available at graduate schools or even through summer programs. Students should also pay attention to the funds allotted to research at particular institutions, which can indicate the extent to which the student can opt for grants to pursue individual research projects.

Tip: Colleges within a university that also hosts graduate programs are more likely to offer more numerous and quality research opportunities.

- Study abroad. The opportunity to spend part of the college period— whether for a semester or a summer—in a different country is very appealing to many students regardless of their academic concentration. Most top colleges offer study abroad programs in countries all over the world. However, some universities require students to arrange their own travel through partner institutions, which can make the planning more difficult. Others place limits on the amount of time a student may spend abroad. Financial aid recipients must pay particular attention to the university's ability to apply the same financial aid to the period the student spends abroad.
- Graduate school placement. If college applicants already envision themselves attending graduate school, they should consider a college's ability to support their preparation for further education. For example, does the college offer the preliminary coursework required to apply for certain graduate degrees? Does the college have a good record of graduates attending programs of interest? Are there advisers in charge of orienting students about graduate school plans and applications?

Tip: Check the college's website for statistics about graduate school placement among former students.

- Libraries. The availability and strength of libraries is essential for an enriching academic experience. In the context of libraries as physical spaces for intellectual study, students should evaluate the number, comfort, and accessibility (proximity and hours of operation) of the libraries at the colleges they are considering. Libraries should also be judged in terms of the quality, quantity, and specialization of their print and electronic collections.

- Legitimacy. Students should only consider universities that have received accreditation, a status that confirms adherence to college-level standards. Attending a school that isn't accredited might prevent students from receiving financial aid or transferring credits to a new university. Searching for recent news about specific universities online is also useful to find out about a university's reputation.

Extracurricular Opportunities

- Student organizations. For many students, participation in extracurricular activities is an essential aspect of the college experience. These students seek colleges with a large number of student-run organizations in a variety of areas and the option to pursue interests that may not be represented by existing organizations. In this respect, it is important to explore opportunities to create new organizations at specific universities, as well as funding available for individual initiatives. On the other hand, the existence and quality of specific groups will be important for students with very defined extracurricular interests. For example, student-athletes will want to attend a university with prestigious teams.

Professional Development

- Recruitment on campus. For a student who wants to increase the chances of landing a good job after graduation, universities' on-campus recruitment initiatives are a must. Many universities foster early interaction between their students and some of the most sought-after companies in the United States and abroad. Through career fairs, networking events, and information sessions on campus, students develop awareness of different industries and have exclusive opportunities to be considered for specific positions.
- Job placement. The effectiveness of universities' employment outreach can be measured through job placement rates. Students should

visit the institutions' websites to access information about the percentage of students gaining employment before or immediately after graduation, the average salaries of recent graduates, and the industries in which these graduates are finding employment at greater rates.

- Career guidance. Universities that are serious about their students' job prospects usually have staff and sometimes even a complete office dedicated to career services. At the very least, students should receive guidance on different career paths and have access to a database of organizations interested in recruiting students from the university.

- Alumni network. A strong alumni network is an excellent resource to find employment. Universities usually facilitate students' interactions with alumni and sometimes even match them according to common backgrounds or professional interests. The presence of an alumni database with options to search alumni by location, professional industry, and specific companies is particularly useful during the job search.

- Internships and fellowships. Many companies distinguish college graduates who have already accumulated some professional experience. Universities can help students gain this experience through internships and fellowships in a variety of fields during the summer or part-time throughout the academic year.

- Local opportunities. Beyond the university campus, students might consider professional opportunities in the local communities. Students with particular career interests may be more attracted to universities located in settings where specific industries are thriving. In turn, local companies usually have ties with nearby academic institutions and are more familiar with their students' training.

Community

- General community. The community is the soul of the university, just like the family is the soul of the home. Even though all universities attract a wide range of people, each community usually has unique characteristics. For example, some communities exhibit more diversity and cohesiveness than others. A university that welcomes students from a wide variety of geographic places and ethnic and religious backgrounds will likely foster a more tolerant and enriching community than a university whose student body is largely homogeneous.

At the same time, a university that cultivates traditions, promotes social interactions among students, and hosts a great volume of programs and events is more likely to showcase a dynamic community in which students bond outside of the classroom. Regardless of the nature of a university's community, students should confirm that they will be surrounded by strong role models—faculty members and other students they want to emulate.

- Sub-communities. Some students look to establish a sense of belonging in specific university groups. For example, many students will place strong value on the existence of certain religious or ethnic networks. Low-income students in particular may want to consider colleges that host the Educational Opportunity Program (EOP), which offers extra academic and personal support to ensure these students complete their college studies successfully.

Tip: Some EOP programs require students to submit a special application to access their services. Through EOP, students may even access waivers toward college application fees and other college-related costs.

Personal Preferences

- Students' personal tastes in areas beyond academics, extracurricular activities, and career interests should not be underestimated. Ideally, the university experience will be fulfilling at every level, and will facilitate personal growth and comfort. Otherwise, students' dissatisfaction with their personal lives may yield negative effects on the overall experience. Some of the factors that students should consider carefully when determining college preferences are climate, proximity to home, school spirit, and accessibility to activities they enjoy pursuing in their spare time.

Accommodation

• For some students, a university's accommodation options are very important. For example, students who have spouses and/or children will value the opportunity to live in independent housing with accessible childcare facilities. Other students may be interested in fraternity or sorority housing. Yet others may long for the experience of living in Harry Potter–style traditional learning communities. And some students will prefer to live off campus, discarding colleges with an on-campus housing requirement. The costs of living on campus versus renting off campus properties should be considered as well.

Coverage of Special Needs

• Some students have medical and other unique conditions that require exceptional attention. These students should ensure that their target colleges are equipped to meet their needs, which usually means the availability of required professionals and appropriate physical and institutional structures. In the case where medical care is needed, colleges must be able to accept existing health insurance or provide their own adequate insurance plans. Applicants should always notify admissions officers of any special needs so they may judge whether the college is prepared or can prepare to welcome the student.

Finances

• Cost of attendance. Low-income students, in particular, will want to pay attention to the full of cost attendance—not just tuition costs—of target institutions. This involves expenses such as lodging, books and other supplies, travel, and health insurance.
• Net price. Students should also pay attention to the actual price they might be attending to attend a specific college. The "net price" is the difference between the full cost of attendance and any financial aid the student expects to receive. Although the net price is just an estimate (as financial aid from the universities is usually not con-

firmed until after the student has been admitted), it is a better predictor of future expenses than the full cost of attendance.

Tip: The College Board website and the U.S. Department of Education's www.collegecost.ed.gov offer a Net Price Calculator that students can use to find out the estimated total costs of attending specific universities. The second website also includes a College Scorecard section with more information about a college's affordability and value, as well as the College Affordability and Transparency List, a section that ranks universities according to their tuition, fees, and net prices.

- Financial aid. As has been previously discussed in this book, the financial aid provided by a university is a better indicator of the actual costs of college for high-achieving, low-income students. These students should aspire to colleges that offer need-based financial aid and need-blind admission.
- Work-study. Even if a university meets a student's full cost of attendance through generous financial aid policies, students would benefit from the availability of work-study programs. A job on campus with a flexible schedule that does not conflict with class time is ideal to generate cash to cover personal expenses.
- Scholarships. Many colleges offer very specific scholarships for which individual students may qualify depending on factors such as ethnic or geographic background, high school GPA, and intended academic concentration. Usually, colleges also accept outside scholarships, or money that students receive from external sources to help them pay the costs of college. The policies governing outside scholarships vary across institutions. Some colleges, for example, will accept these awards to reduce students' expected payments only to a certain limit. If the amount of the scholarship exceeds this limit, the colleges may reduce the provided financial aid by an equal amount.

Once students have created a list of critical characteristics, many struggle to determine which are more important than others. Weighing preferences regarding college is important because students are unlikely to find institutions that exhibit all critical characteristics. Of course, the relative value of the critical characteristics will depend on the student's personal situation. Those aspiring to become scientists, for example, will place strong value on the opportunity to conduct scientific research, while this opportunity might go unnoticed for students interested in the humanities and social sciences.

However, if we take into consideration that the greatest benefit of a college education is to undergo integral learning—growing socially and academically—all students would do well to prioritize the strength of the academics and the motivation and preparation of the student body. For all students from low-income families, moreover, the financial access should also be a top-ranked characteristic.

STRATEGIES TO EXPLORE COLLEGES

As can be inferred from the previous section, choosing target colleges is a largely introspective process. Only after students have seriously defined their preferences regarding college—arguably one of the most important periods of their lives—will they be prepared to choose the specific institutions to which they will submit applications for admission.

At this point, how does a student find a few colleges with different selectivity matching the identified set of preferences? A good starting point is the College Search tool available on the College Board's website. This tool lets students filter the search according to helpful categories such as location, majors, and test scores. The U.S. Department of Education's College Scorecard website (collegescorecard.ed.gov) also includes a useful directory to compare colleges based on factors such as average annual costs, graduation rates, and salary of recent graduates.

Some students may turn to popular college ranking lists published by sources such as *U.S. News and World Report*. Yet, they should take these rankings with more than a grain of salt. It is very likely that the criteria used to order the institutions will differ from the characteristics of critical importance to individual students.

U.S. News, for example, based its 2014 list of best colleges on seven main categories: undergraduate academic reputation, graduation and retention rates, faculty resources, student selectivity, financial resources, alumni giving, and graduation rate performance (the difference between the expected and actual graduation rates for students entering in a specific year).[2] These factors are almost exclusively academic. They do not account for student preferences in non-academic areas such as athletics, student organizations, housing, or location. And the relative weight they assign to each category may also differ from student priorities.

A second problem with these rankings is the difficulty in measuring intangible qualities such as reputation. *U.S. News* evaluates the latter through an annual survey that is sent to high university officials and some high school representatives, asking them to rate the academic programs of peer institutions on a scale from one to five. As one can easily infer, outsiders are unlikely to be so familiar with an institution's current academics as to provide a fair assessment.

On the other hand, the participants' memory or prejudices may also interfere with the legitimacy of the rankings, assigning a university a value that it has historically obtained or a value the participant deems it "should" obtain given the popular perception of the university. In any case, the implicit idea that a university's reputation is established by the opinion of academic figures alone is highly debatable. The extent to which specific universities meet workforce needs, for example, should also be taken into account.

Recently, new private organizations and even the U.S. government have begun to challenge existing university rankings and to provide their own alternatives, focusing on a different set of criteria. *MONEY* magazine, for example, has generated a lot of buzz with a list of 665 colleges evaluated against three categories: educational quality, affordability, and alumni earnings.

Unlike other sources, *MONEY* takes into account colleges' net price to assess affordability, and follows the growing belief that universities should be judged based on the financial success of recent graduates. Babson College, Webb Institute, MIT, Princeton, and Stanford occupied the top five places of this new rank.

In general, all college rankings are inaccurate because they do not show which universities are better *for each individual student*, a task that only the applicants themselves are able to undertake after carefully analyzing what they expect to get out of a college education. The *U.S. News* and similar lists should thus be used only as another filter of accredited institutions of higher learning, not as a perfect report on the institutions' relative quality.

After conducting the preliminary college search through general on-line directories, students will have a list of institutions that seemingly meet the established characteristics of critical importance. In order to explore these institutions in more detail, however, students should turn to the institutions' official websites. The latter usually offer a vast amount of information that may overwhelm a first-time visitor. To facil-itate the investigation, students should start by visiting the undergradu-ate admissions page. This, in turn, will generally include links to other important sections such as the different academic departments, the course catalogue, and the directory of student organizations.

Tip: College admissions officers equate mastery of the official website's content with the applicant's interest in the college. Prospective students should therefore spend significant time familiarizing themselves with target colleges' websites, and avoid asking college representatives any information clearly explained there.

Once students have finished the detailed research of each shortlisted college, it would be ideal to conduct campus visits before submitting applications for admission. Let's return to the dating analogy for a sec-ond. Even in today's hyper-connected society, where romantic relation-ships flourish online more and more frequently, nothing beats the pow-er of the physical encounter. The kind of chemistry sparked through personal interactions is impossible to replicate through the phone or the computer screen.

Confirming attraction toward a particular college is no different. It is not until we sit in a lecture hall, walk through the campus, and chat with current students and professors that we can sense the presence or ab-sence of a true *fit*. Some families are unable to afford the costs of visiting even just one college campus, and it is okay if they don't, as colleges will not hold this against applicants.

Students should still consider the various opportunities to visit col-leges at no cost even before submitting an application. Many high schools organize college tours throughout the academic year. There are also several community-based organizations such as QuestBridge that coordinate campus tours for low-income students. Finally, some of the top universities themselves invite a select group of high school students for a free campus visit (usually known as "fly-in" programs).

*Tip: Students should be aware that their behavior during college cam-
pus visits will be taken into consideration during the evaluation for
admission, even if the visit takes place before students submit an official
application. Visitors should thus conduct themselves with politeness at
all times. They should demonstrate their interest in the institution and
take advantage of any opportunity to speak with professors, current
students, and admissions representatives to learn more about the university and the college experience in general. Any misbehavior could
seriously undermine the student's chances of being admitted into the
college.*

The following are a sample of visiting programs that pay all travel
costs so prospective students can explore firsthand some of the nation's
most selective colleges:

- Diversity Hosting Weekend, College of Engineering, Cornell
  University
- Diversity Open Houses, Amherst College
- Discover Middlebury, Middlebury College
- Barnard Bound, Barnard College
- Discover Wellesley Travel Grant, Wellesley College

Visiting Harvard, actually experiencing life on its campus during senior fall was determinant to verify my interests regarding college. Now
I knew I definitely wanted to attend a residential university where
the housing system was a central part of the learning and social
environment. I knew I was seeking a vibrant institution that featured
rigorous academics and a wide array of extracurricular activities. And
I wanted a place where I could study and live with talented, passion-
ate students from the most diverse backgrounds.

Given our limited resources, my parents could not have afforded
to pay the cost of an extensive college campus tour. I therefore took
advantage of the unique opportunity to be hosted by David, my
mentor, seeing it as a chance not just to explore Harvard, but also to
examine the elements that shape the college experience in general.

8

APPLYING FOR COLLEGE ADMISSION
What It Takes and How to Do It for Free

The end of junior year in high school signals the start of the college admissions cycle. Universities begin to post applications on their websites. Rising seniors find their mailboxes increasingly filled with informational materials from different institutions. Teachers start getting requests for letters of reference. And many families flock to college campuses all throughout the country for tours and info sessions, hoping to identify the perfect match for their sons and daughters.

This is the moment every college aspirant has been awaiting. The students who have taken advantage of every academic and extracurricular opportunity can now maximize the possibility to convey their extraordinary interest and aptitude through every component of the application. College may still seem distant—after all, it is still two summers and a full academic year away. And yet, the application timeline and complexity of the process demand that students start preparing more than a year in advance.

The task can appear daunting. There are multiple deadlines to manage, at least one long essay to write, and the pressure to keep track of several documents that both the student and school need to submit to individual universities. Yet, students who have pursued a rigorous high school curriculum and excelled in activities beyond the classroom should not worry too much. *These students are already considered competitive applicants to the top universities in the country.*

The challenge ahead is to communicate individual achievements and qualities strategically to their target colleges, meeting every application requirement by the designated deadlines. With early and careful planning, applying to college can be stress-free.

This process can also be *free*. Although in theory universities charge fees for the submission of every application, this chapter will provide valuable tips so that students with limited economic resources can apply to their dream colleges at no cost.

APPLICATION REQUIREMENTS

Even though selective colleges have similar application processes, every university has unique requirements. As soon as students have defined their targets they should visit the official undergraduate admissions websites and check the specific materials required by each institution. Usually, the undergraduate admissions page will also include information for transfer and visiting candidates. High school seniors should pay attention only to the freshman, or first-year, requirements.

Tips: When searching for application guidelines on universities' admissions websites, students should look for any blogs by admissions officers or current students. These blogs, as well as the admissions offices' Twitter and Facebook accounts, usually contain updated information on the application process as well as helpful tips from the same people who make admissions decisions.

Most selective universities will require the following documents:

Main Application Forms

Every college asks students to submit personal information such as contact details, parent occupations, high school courses and extracurriculars, summer activities, and standardized testing results. Whereas some universities have their own application forms, others accept a standard application that students can fill only once and submit to more than one target college.

There are two main types of standard application: the Common Application and the Universal College Application. As of the summer of 2015, over five hundred colleges from the United States (as well as Austria, France, Germany, Italy, United Kingdom, and Switzerland) accepted the Common Application. Only over forty colleges almost exclusively from the United States were subscribed to the Universal College Application, though membership has been steadily increasing.

The Common and Universal applications are very similar, with only subtle differences. If a student's target colleges are subscribed to both standard applications, the student should pick just one of the two, but never submit both to the same institutions. Colleges that accept both applications usually have no preference for one or the other. Students should pick the one to which most of their targets colleges are subscribed.

Tip: Students find the Common Application at www.commonapp.org and the Universal College Application at www.universalcollegeapp.com.

Although the Common and Universal apps are the most popular standard applications in the country, students should be aware of regional standard applications as well. For example, many universities located in Texas require students to submit the single standard application called ApplyTexas. Specific universities will indicate in their websites which standard applications, if any, they accept.

University Supplements

Many universities subscribed to standard applications will still require applicants to fill out additional forms specific to each institution. These individual forms are called *university supplements*, and they usually include essay prompts. Whereas all target colleges receive the content that students fill in the standard applications, the supplements are sent only to the specific institutions. Students who choose to submit the Common App may find the supplements in one section of this standard application. If they choose to fill out the Universal College Application, they should look for the supplements in the universities' admissions websites and follow their individual submission guidelines.

Standardized Test Scores

Normally, selective universities require applicants to submit scores from the SAT or ACT, and from the SAT Subject Tests. As mentioned earlier in this book, some universities are starting to make these exams optional, or eliminating the requirement altogether, but the tests nonetheless remain one of the most important indicators of applicants' academic aptitude. Taking standardized tests also gives students advantages outside of the admissions process. For example, high-scorers may be able to graduate from college earlier (depending on the institution), or qualify for certain scholarships and college-prep programs.

What Do the ACT and SAT Test?

The ACT and SAT are very similar exams. Both are divided into timed sections that test the reading comprehension, writing, and math skills that students should have acquired by eleventh grade. Unlike the SAT, the ACT also contains a science section, which tests students on analysis of scientific information presented in the form of graphs, tables, and descriptions of experiments and hypotheses. In addition, students have the option to take the ACT with or without the writing test, a thirty-minute essay comparable to the required fifty-minute essay found on the SAT. Most selective universities ask that applicants take the version of the ACT that includes the writing test (formally called "ACT Plus Writing").

Colleges normally consider the ACT and SAT as equivalent, and allow applicants to submit scores from either exam. It is thus strategic to take both tests and submit the scores from the exam in which the student has delivered a better performance. Students who obtain high scores in both exams would do well to submit the results of both.

What Are the SAT Subject Tests?

The SAT Subject Tests are one-hour exams that allow students to demonstrate mastery of specific subjects in five general academic areas: history, foreign languages, English, mathematics, and science. While not every university requires these exams, high-achieving students aspiring to the top colleges should take at least two to confirm competency in specific disciplines. Like other standardized tests such as AP, IB, and A Levels, the SAT Subject Tests help universities determine whether applicants are prepared for certain majors and even freshman-year courses. Likewise, strong performance in SAT Subject Tests in languages can allow students to fulfill the foreign language requirement at certain colleges, or study the language at a more advanced level.

In order to select the SAT Subject Tests the student will take, it is important to check if the target colleges require specific ones. MIT applicants, for example, must submit one Subject Test in math and one in science. If the target colleges have no preference regarding Subject Tests, applicants should take the tests in the academic areas in which they feel most confident.

In any case, students should avoid presenting more than one test in the same academic area; for example, they should not submit scores for both Math Level I and Math Level II. At the same time, colleges prefer that students do not take Subject Tests in their native languages, if other than English, as language Subject Tests are designed to test skills in foreign language learning.

Tip: Students can register for the ACT at www.actstudent.org, and for the SAT and SAT Subject Tests at www.collegeboard.org. Both websites contain detailed information about each exam as well as free test preparation materials.

When Should Students Take Standardized Exams?

The SAT, ACT, and Subject Tests are offered multiple times throughout the academic year and students can take them at any point in their high school period. However, in order to take the scores into consideration during the admissions process, most colleges require applicants to submit score reports to them by the fall of senior year. This means students should plan to take the exams with enough time in advance of the college application deadlines.

Given that these exams can be taken more than once, it is especially important to leave plenty of time for at least a second sitting, in which students many times obtain higher scores. Another point to consider is that the SAT and the SAT Subject Tests are offered on the same dates, and students may only take one or the other during the same administration. Because the exams are usually offered only once a month, it takes a student at least two months to complete both.

The ideal moment to take each standardized exam varies by individ-ual. Most applicants to selective universities begin to take the exams in the spring of their junior year and finish by November of their senior year. However, some students are prepared to deliver a strong perfor-mance on the exams much earlier, even during the freshman or sopho-more years, and prefer to get the exams out of the way before their academic schedules become more rigorous and they acquire more ex-tracurricular responsibilities.

In the case of SAT Subject Tests, it is advised that students take them at the same time they are studying the same subjects in school. For example, a student who has recently completed the AP U.S. Histo-ry curriculum will be more likely to obtain a good score on the equiva-lent Subject Test than someone who has not studied the same material or has already forgotten it.

How to Report Standardized Test Scores to Colleges

Although both the Common Application and Universal College Appli-cation let students list their standardized test scores in their respective forms, students must request for the College Board and ACT to send official score reports to each target institution. Both testing agencies allow all students to send up to four score reports at no cost. In order to benefit from this opportunity, students must select the four recipients during the registration for each exam, or up to nine days after the Saturday test date in the case of the SAT and SAT Subject Tests. *In addition to these four score reports, students who qualify for an SAT fee waiver get four additional score reports.*

In order to maximize the number of score reports that can be sent at no cost, students who take both the ACT and SAT can consider sending ACT scores to a set of colleges and SAT scores to a different set of colleges. This strategy is only applicable when all recipients accept ei-ther the SAT or the ACT, and when students have performed at a similar level in both exams. Some colleges specifically ask that students who have taken both the SAT and the ACT submit *both* score sets.

When reporting SAT and SAT Subject Test scores to colleges, stu-dents should also be aware of the opportunity granted by the College Board to choose which specific scores to send. For example, a student may have obtained outstanding math and reading scores and a poor writing score in the first SAT sitting. If the student decides to retake the exam and obtains a higher score in writing but not in math and reading, some colleges accept a combined report that contains individual scores from multiple test dates (in this case, for example, the reading and math scores from the first sitting, and the writing score from the second sitting).

Students who take Subject Tests can also choose which individual exam scores to send to colleges. The College Board officially calls this score selection policy Score Choice. Students should note that not all colleges accept Score Choice. Stanford, for example, requires applicants to submit scores from *all* test dates. It is thus imperative that students read very carefully the standardized testing requirements of each target college. Unlike the College Board, the ACT does not combine scores from different test dates in score reports. An ACT score report will only contain ACT scores from a single test date.

Tip: Students who qualify for an SAT fee waiver get four score reports at no cost (in addition to the four score reports every student receives when they register to take an exam). These additional score reports can be sent to colleges at any time. Therefore, eligible students can wait to receive their scores before they decide which specific ones they send to colleges that accept Score Choice. Some schools such as Brown also accept SAT and ACT scores as official if they are printed directly on the high school transcript, making it unnecessary to submit reports through the College Board. Students should thus persuade their schools to reflect standardized test scores on the transcripts and ask all target colleges if they would accept this reporting method.

Essays

Both the Common and Universal Apps include a writing section, which the applicant must fill with a personal essay, or statement, of no more than 650 words. Some university supplements also require additional essays with a variety of prompts and word limits. The purpose of these sections is not merely to test the applicant's writing skills, which are already demonstrated through grades in high school English classes and standardized test scores. More importantly, the universities take advantage of this opportunity to get to know the students at a more personal level, capturing their voice, their values, and their priorities in life.

Tip: In contrast to what many believe, college application essays DO get read, and very carefully. They are an integral part of the evaluation process.

Many terrific applicants make the mistake of neglecting the weight of the essays in admissions decisions and submit responses that do not honor their qualities to the greatest extent possible. When admissions officers receive essays that have been written carelessly, or whose quality falls below the level expected of someone with high grades in English and in reading and writing tests, they may interpret it as a sign of disinterest in the college. In turn, admissions officers may be willing to give an applicant with lower than expected grades and scores more favorable consideration if the applicant submits outstanding personal statements.

In the context of these statements, the key word is "personal." Students will notice that prompts usually encourage them to recall experiences of special significance to their development into the person they are today. The 2014–2015 Universal College Application, for example, offered the following topic ideas: "a person you admire; a life-changing experience; or your viewpoint on a particular current event." The Common Application for the same admissions cycle provided actual prompts for students to choose from, but the topics were equally broad and introspective:

- Some students have a background or story that is so central to their identity that they believe their application would be incomplete without it. If this sounds like you, then please share your story.
- Recount an incident or time when you experienced failure. How did it affect you, and what lessons did you learn?
- Reflect on a time when you challenged a belief or idea. What prompted you to act? Would you make the same decision again?
- Describe a place or environment where you are perfectly content. What do you do or experience there, and why is it meaningful to you?

- Discuss an accomplishment or event—formal or informal—that marked your transition from childhood to adulthood within your culture, community, or family.

Many students dread the college essays, uncertain about the "right" content and tone. Although in theory the personal nature of the prompts would allow any student to develop them based on individual experiences, some students wonder if their life stories will actually seem interesting to admissions officers. Other students worry that the strict word limit makes it impossible to write a meaningful essay, especially if the student would like to share multiple experiences, all equally significant to him or her.

Whenever anxiety about the college essays arises among students, they should be encouraged to appreciate the extraordinary and often neglected opportunities presented by this application component. If you think about it, students have a very limited chance to show their full potential throughout most of the application process. Application forms ask really specific questions, leaving little space to elaborate on individual circumstances. In the same way, the format of standardized exams places value on speed and accuracy, ignoring the ingenuity and sophisticated thinking through which students may have arrived at the correct results.

These are examples of the way in which admissions offices decide which information is most relevant to make admissions decisions. The essays, however, provide a rare chance for applicants to determine which information about themselves should also be considered when assessing their candidacy. Students should see the writing sections as a blank canvas on which they can paint, in the most beautiful palette available, the attributes that make them worthy of admission into their target colleges.

Above all, applicants must welcome the college essay as an opportunity to showcase their uniqueness. Many students will have similar backgrounds, participate in similar extracurricular activities, and obtain similar grades and test scores. The best way to ensure a student's application stands out from the rest is to write an essay that nobody else but the student could have written—an essay so authentic, so true to the student's essence, that admissions officers will remember it even after having read a thousand others. The only way to craft such a unique and memorable text is to make it really personal. After all, nobody else shares one's specific experiences.

Students should not stress over the perceived worth of these experiences. An effective essay does not depend on how exotic or sensational a student life has been. College admissions officers are not expecting applicants to write about their travels abroad, monumental achievements in sports or academics, or dramatic life events such as surviving natural catastrophes or illness.

Applicants will never be judged negatively for the lack of experiences that were outside of their reach. Besides, many of the most effective college essays touch on seemingly ordinary or insignificant moments that have nonetheless elicited an important transformation in the way the student thinks and acts. It may be the challenging journey through a particular class in high school, the origin of the student's professional vocation, the lessons learned from participating in rewarding community activities, or the impact of a relationship with a mentor, a teacher, or a family member. More than the specific topic, what matters is that the writing reflects, compellingly and honestly, the human being behind the application.

Such an effective self-portrayal usually results from a balance of spontaneous prose and meticulous revision. On the one hand, students should strive to reflect their authentic voices, writing as if they were engaging in a very personal monologue with an attentive, educated, and genuinely interested audience. Like in an actual conversation, employing overly contrived language and seeking to impress the audience with vocabulary will make it difficult to communicate the main message, and students risk appearing like a very different person.

Spontaneity, however, should not be confused with carelessness. It is equally distracting and disrespectful to the audience to present mistakes in spelling and grammar, or to pick offensive or excessively intimate topics. To ensure the personal statements are both authentic and appropriate in the context of college admissions, applicants should conduct several editing rounds and request feedback from people who know them well such as family members, friends, and teachers. A college essay is effective if a student's close ones recognize the student's distinctive voice throughout the text.

I began to write my own college essays the summer before my senior year. In late July I had already completed the first draft of my main Common Application essay, and I was not happy with the result. I remember writing about my family's migration from Cuba through an extended metaphor that presented me as a sailor on a voyage. The idea was not terrible (though definitely not very original) but I focused so much on developing the metaphor that I had a hard time shedding light on the real implications of our journey to the United States. After seeking feedback from my parents and guidance counselor, I decided to start from scratch.

After many attempts, I wrote a very straightforward essay about the lessons of perseverance I had learned from my mother as she sought to validate her medical degree in our new country. My language was simple, and the imagery even more so. I actually evoked just a single image throughout the four or five paragraphs: my parents, my sister, and I gathering around our dinner table every night to focus on our respective academic tasks. And yet, my message was powerful: a united, dedicated family could move forward in the United States despite the lack of resources, the language barriers, and the difficult assimilation into a new culture. Using my mother's struggles as a lens to explore our story, I communicated to my target universities that I placed a very strong value on hard work, family ties, and education.

It is worth cautioning that the topic of my personal statement should not necessarily incline others to write similar essays, as if it were a formula. My essay was authentic and relevant given my particular family circumstances, and it worked because I wrote about what was truly important to me. And yet, it did not come easily. The first draft was not good enough. Nor were the second or third. It was only after I had written four or five versions and received extensive feedback from my close ones throughout the course of three months that I decided I was done.

Supplemental Materials

Some students have truly exceptional talents they cannot fully represent in the standard college application. There are, for example, prominent musicians, scientists conducting groundbreaking research, or distinguished painters who may want colleges to review their work. Most selective colleges welcome this additional and completely optional information—officially called supplemental or supplementary materials—to help them conduct a more effective evaluation of unique candidates. Before they pick these materials, students should pay close attention to the submission guidelines published in the universities' undergraduate admissions websites. Some institutions have very strict requirements regarding the format and nature of the materials they accept.

Tip: Students should create a "College Application" folder in a computer desktop, and sub-folders for each target college. These folders will be helpful to organize all relevant documents such as personal statements, scholarship applications, forms, and supplementary materials.

Recommendation Letters

It is very helpful for universities to have teachers confirm the applicant's readiness for college. Given that admissions officers rarely have the chance to meet applicants in person, the teachers' insights into the students' academic performance, personality, and general high school trajectory are extremely valuable. Most selective universities therefore request that applicants submit letters of recommendation from teachers that know them well. Different institutions ask for a different number of recommendations, while some even specify the kind of teacher that should provide a reference. MIT, for example, requests a letter from a math or science teacher and one from a humanities, social science, or language teacher.

There are a few tips to maximize the value of the letters of recommendation. Ideally, the recommenders will have taught the student in a core academic class in the sciences, social studies, mathematics, or languages. Colleges usually prefer letters from teachers who taught the student in eleventh grade, since this is the most recent academic year the student will have completed before applying to college.

Teachers who taught the student only in ninth or tenth grade may have an outdated view of the student's academic and personal development, whereas teachers who meet students in twelfth grade will not have enough time to really get to know them before the college application deadlines in the fall and winter. Of course, teachers who have taught a student in multiple academic years, including eleventh grade, can usually provide the most effective descriptions of the student's long-term development.

Students should secure recommendations from teachers familiar not only with the students' academic skills but also with their personality and involvement in activities outside of classes. Outstanding letters include specific anecdotes that illustrate the student's qualities as a classmate and positive member of the wider community. One common mistake is to select teachers based on their perceived prestige or because it was in their class that students obtained the highest grades. If the teachers don't know the students well enough, it is likely they will write a generic letter that will not do justice to the applicant's strengths. Like the college essays, the letters should be so personal that they could not have been written for any other student.

Certainly, students do not have control over the content of the recommendation letters—and they should refuse some teachers' dishonorable requests to have the students write their own letters, later signed by the teacher. What applicants can do is provide teachers detailed information about their activities, academic plans, and personal circumstances so that recommenders can reflect a deeper understanding of the applicant in their letters.

Students should also give recommenders plenty of time to write the letters, as it is much more difficult to write a compelling text when deadlines are imminent. Finally, it is ideal to pick teachers who are familiar with different aspects of a student's background so that the letters do not repeat but rather complement each other.

In some cases, students may feel there is someone beyond the required teachers who could provide colleges a valuable recommendation on the student's behalf. Although some universities explicitly ask students not to submit materials beyond what is requested, many do welcome additional references that may help them assess the candidate. In these cases, however, applicants should be careful not to submit a letter that merely repeats the content already present in the required letters. At the same time, students should avoid bombarding admissions offices with too many materials; usually, no more than one extra reference, if at all, should be sent.

School Reports

Besides the teacher recommendations, colleges also request another school official to submit a more detailed report about the applicant's academic history. Officially called the School Report, this form is available through both the Common and Universal College Applications and is usually filled by the college or guidance counselor (although it can also be submitted by another member of the school administration with access to the student's records). The report asks for information about the student's current schedule, class rank, and GPA, as well as the school's academic policies. It also requires the submission of an official transcript, and provides the option to submit an extended written evaluation of the applicant.

Tip: Counselors or other school officials unfamiliar with the student's history might not be able to provide an evaluation that otherwise would have been helpful. Students should therefore strive to build close relationships with guidance counselors and school officials as early as possible in their high school career.

Some students wonder how universities will know the level of difficulty of the academic curriculum they have pursued in high school. In some schools, for example, there are no standardized curricula such as AP or IB, yet the classes offered are at least as rigorous. The School Report allows colleges to gain a more accurate picture of the student's level of preparation and the extent to which he or she has maximized the opportunities to attain as good an education as possible given the resources available at the school.

The School Report should be submitted to target colleges along with the rest of the standard application materials. However, universities will still require updated reports on student's performance throughout senior year. For this purpose, students should submit the official Midyear Report and Final Report available at both the Common and Universal Apps. The latter also includes a First Marking Period Report to be submitted after the School Report.

Tip: Applicants who have attended more than one high school should submit a School Report from each.

Résumé or Curriculum Vitae

The limited space available in the college applications to describe students' activities and achievements motivates some to submit an additional document containing their academic and extracurricular history in detail. This document is commonly known as a curriculum vitae (CV) and its shorter version is called a résumé. Some colleges will actually require a CV or résumé as part of the application, and the Common App allows students to attach a résumé when a specific university asks for it. Other universities will let students send the résumé via e-mail or regular mail, whereas a few prohibit the submission of this document altogether.

In the event the applicant's target colleges welcome or at least do not prohibit the submission of a CV or résumé, and if the student feels there is certainly not enough space in the application forms to reflect important milestones, then this additional document can be very helpful. For example, it can serve to describe in detail the student's work experience, activities conducted during school breaks, multiple awards, and even interesting hobbies.

The document, however, should not be so long that it distracts the attention of the admissions officers, and it should reflect the substance of the activities and achievements described rather than just providing a laundry list. It is always important to check colleges' admissions websites for any specific guidelines regarding the format of additional documentation.

As I was applying to college, I realized the space allotted in the application forms was not enough to include all my activities. David, my mentor, suggested I send a resume, and lent me his so that I could copy the format. The funny part is that David himself had borrowed this format from a friend who used it to apply to a fast food restaurant. At the end of the day, the format of the document didn't really matter. All I had to make sure was that I was sharing with colleges new content in a concise way, reflecting my varied interests and the main impact of my extracurriculars.

Tip: A good CV or résumé usually includes the following sections: Name and Contact Information; Education (high schools, location, period of attendance, standardized test scores, class rank, academic programs outside of school, and advanced courses such as AP and IB); Extracurricular Activities (organizations, results, and impact of individual participation and leadership positions); Academic and Non-Academic Awards; Professional Experience (employer, length of work experience, primary responsibilities, and results); Special Skills (examples: computer programming and foreign languages); International Experience (living and/or studying abroad) and Hobbies.

Application Fees

One factor that usually limits the number of colleges to which students end up applying is the application fee. As mentioned earlier in this book, most universities, especially the selective ones, require applicants to pay a fee usually ranging from thirty to almost one hundred dollars at the time they submit the application forms. Yet there are ways to obtain application fee waivers that allow students to apply to colleges at no cost:

- College Board Application Fee Waivers. The students who have used the College Board's fee waiver service to take the SAT and SAT Subject Tests can also obtain up to four fee waivers to apply to college for free. According to the College Board's official website, these students should receive the Request for Waiver of College Application Fee automatically after they take the exams. However, students who do not receive them can still submit a request directly to their schools' guidance counselors. Note that these fee waivers are accepted only at institutions listed on the SAT Fee-Waiver Directory of Colleges, also available on the College Board's website.
- NACAC Application Fee Waiver. Students with limited economic resources may also qualify for the National Association for College Admission Counseling's (NACAC) fee waivers. For a complete list of the circumstances that make a student eligible for this benefit, visit the official NACAC website, www.nacacnet.org.
- Universities' fee waivers. Some institutions offer their own fee waivers with their own eligibility criteria. If this information is not

readily available on the official admissions website, students should still check with target colleges by phone or e-mail as sometimes they are willing to waive the fee on a case-by-case basis. Whenever a student is requesting fee waivers without an official College Board or NACAC form, it helps to have a guidance counselor support the student's request by writing a note that explains the student's financial hardship.

Tip: Students may qualify for both the NACAC and College Board fee waivers. As such, eligible students may use the College Board fee waivers to apply to four colleges and the NACAC waivers to apply to additional institutions.

The College Board's recent Realize Your College Potential (RYCP) initiative promises to reduce college application costs further for students from low-income families. Through RYCP, the College Board will send high-achieving high school seniors a packet that includes customized application tips, information on college net costs and four-year graduation rates, a sample college list, and *eight* college application fee waivers accepted by 150 selective colleges.

One final opportunity to reduce college application costs is to submit application forms online instead of sending the same documents in print by mail. Some universities will lower or eliminate application fees for students submitting the forms through their admissions websites.

Tip: Students may also consider establishing a special college fund at their high schools, raising money to help seniors who cannot afford the college application fees.

All the hard work that goes into assembling the numerous application materials will pay off once students officially submit them to the target colleges. The rewarding feeling of accomplishment should be cherished, even though it will inevitably mix with the anxiety that will deepen as one approaches the date in which colleges announce their admissions decisions. During this waiting period, however, applicants will also have to take a care of a few matters related to the application process:

- Tracking application materials. If universities have not confirmed receipt of all required materials in the two weeks following the submission of the application, students should contact the admissions offices. I personally know students who have received rejection letters because the universities claimed a complete application was never submitted, when in fact it had.
- Sharing significant updates. Whereas the Midyear Report sent by school officials will already communicate to colleges the most recent grades and GPA, applicants can also send institutions a brief letter describing particular achievements in academics and extracurriculars that took place after the application forms were submitted. Students should ensure that all communication with colleges is relevant to the admissions process and remains succinct. Unnecessary or excessive letters, e-mails, or phone calls from an applicant can actually hurt the latter's admissions chances.
- Preparing for interviews. Many universities require applicants or give them the option to attend an interview as part of the evaluation process. The college interviews are usually conducted in the applicant's hometown by a former student of the college that lives in the local area. However, they may also take place through an online chat or even at the college campus, if the student happens to visit or resides nearby.

Many applicants dread the interview almost as much as they dread the college essays, anticipating an intimidating question-and-answer session that will put them to the test from the second it starts. But most college interviews couldn't be farther from this image. Applicants might not realize that local interviewers are hoping that more students from their hometown graduate from their alma mater; these interviewers seek to present the students in the most favorable light in the evaluation letters they send to admissions offices once the interview is over.

On the other hand, interviews are normally very informal. Interviewers will rarely have a defined set of questions or expect students to provide "right answers." The applicant should engage actively in the conversation and see the interview as an opportunity to learn more about the college from the perspective of the interviewer.

Given the informal nature of interviews, there is little the applicant can do to prepare for them. Questions can cover an infinite number of topics, including, for example, the applicant's interest in the college, academic and professional plans, extracurricular activities, family history, opinion about current affairs, preferred books, or anything that the interviewer may deem important.

Some interviewers can also get very creative with their questions. During his Harvard interview, one of my good friends had to answer whether he would prefer to be an apple or a pear, and justify his decision. Another one of my Harvard classmates had an interviewer who asked to conduct the conversation in the applicant's bedroom to determine how his surroundings reflected his interests and personality. I personally attended interviews at alumni's work offices and private homes, and had phone interviews as well. Every interview provided a great chance to explain my background and aspirations more clearly, and to ask very specific questions about the interviewers' respective campus experience.

Here are some interview tips college applicants have found helpful in the past:

- Research the address of the meeting place beforehand to avoid being late (which happened to me for my Yale interview)
- Bring a copy of your résumé the interviewer can keep as a reference
- Dress appropriately, avoiding sneakers, shorts, flip-flops, and tank tops (very formal suits including jackets or ties are not necessary though)
- Research the university in detail and prepare legitimate questions about content that does not appear on university publications
- Be prepared to answer questions about current national and international affairs

APPLICATION TIMELINE

Applying to college successfully means submitting all required materials *and* doing it on time. Colleges maintain very strict deadlines, which vary across institutions. As soon as applicants select their target colleges, they should thus create a calendar in which they post every important deadline, which in turn can be found on colleges' admissions websites. At the same time, it is important to plan to send all materials well in advance of the deadlines to account for potential events that may delay the process.

Tip: Applicants might find it useful to design a special weekly schedule that indicates specific days and times that will be devoted to work on specific components of the application. It also helps to partner with fellow college applicants and meet for weekly group sessions to brainstorm essay topics, study for standardized exams, prepare for the interview, discuss target colleges, and share helpful tips and encouragement.

Despite the fact that specific application deadlines vary from college to college, most universities offer two main application rounds on similar dates—the Early round in October or November and the Regular Action round in December or January. Students who choose to apply to college during the Early round can do so under one of two categories: Early Action and Early Decision. Some colleges, however, only offer one of the two categories, if at all.

Early Action applicants must submit all application materials just a couple of months into their senior year, and usually receive an admissions decision before the Regular Action deadline. However, they may still apply to other universities via Regular Action and choose to attend any of them. Some institutions allow students to apply to multiple colleges under the Early Action category. Others, however, offer what is called "Restrictive Early Action," a version of this application round that does not allow students to apply to more than one college early.

Early Decision applicants also apply to colleges early, around October or November of twelfth grade. However, this application round is *binding*, the term used by colleges to describe the Early Decision applicants' obligation to attend the college that accepts them under this category. Applicants must thus withdraw their applications to any other colleges if their Early Decision institution accepts them.

The benefits of each application round depend on the particular circumstances of individual applicants. Applying early works well for students who have accumulated strong academic and extracurricular records already and are not relying on senior-year achievements to make them competitive candidates. It also works for students with a clear preference for specific colleges, who would be happy to avoid the process of applying to more colleges later in the year.

Many students are drawn to the Early round because fewer students apply then, and the percentage of students admitted is usually larger than the Regular Action rate. Nonetheless, prospective students should take into account that early applicants are also the most competitive. In most cases, students ready to apply early present stronger credentials and have received more support throughout the application than those who apply later in the year. Thus, only very good applicants can be certain to benefit from the higher admissions rates during the Early round.

Early Decision applicants have an even greater probability of getting in than do Early Action applicants, because colleges prefer students they are sure will accept their offer of admission. However, students should decide to apply via Early Decision only when they are absolutely convinced that they would not prefer to attend any other college. Low-income students might find it difficult to decide the best college option for them before they are able to compare multiple offers. It is not until students receive acceptance letters that they learn about the specific financial aid and other benefits they can obtain at different colleges.

When a student applies to college early, he or she can be accepted, rejected, or deferred. The third option means the applicant will be evaluated again during Regular Action, along with the rest of the students who apply during that round. After Regular Action evaluations are conducted, applicants may be accepted, rejected, or placed on a waitlist. Regular Action decisions are usually announced in March and April, and students have until early May to communicate their responses to colleges.

No single application timeline is ideal for everybody. Students must carefully assess their admissions probabilities, the time it will take to prepare application materials, and their relative interest in every target college to decide whether it makes sense for them to apply via Early Action, Early Decision, or Regular Action. In general, however, competitive applicants benefit from applying Early Action to at least one college, and to the rest of the target colleges during Regular Action. That way, they ensure they are benefitting from higher admissions rates during the early round and maximizing the opportunity to compare different college offers.

Coming from a family with few economic resources, submitting the college applications was just one part of the process. Parallel to it, I focused my efforts on securing funding, both from the universities themselves and external organizations, ensuring that I could afford the colleges that would accept me. The next chapter will explain how I went about requesting and obtaining enough financial aid to pay for college and even meet other related costs.

9

SECURING FINANCIAL AID TO PAY FOR COLLEGE

One of the main objectives of this book is to explain why some of the country's most selective universities are also the most affordable for students from low-income families. Chapter 2 describes the financial aid policies that allow universities like Brown, Columbia, Yale, and the University of Pennsylvania to retain students whose families make less money annually than the official yearly cost of attendance at these institutions.

But how does one actually get this available aid? How can students secure extra money from other organizations when our target colleges' financial aid packages are not enough? What kinds of financial aid are there? And when is the right time to submit financial aid applications?

This chapter will answer these and many other important financial aid questions which students are likely to consider during the college application process. It will suggest concrete actions to secure as much aid as possible, and show that it is never too early to begin the process.

> As a senior in high school, I received about $200,000 dollars destined to help me pay the costs of attending college. Most of this generous financial aid came from Harvard, but other organizations that host independent scholarship programs also contributed substantially. Without their combined help I never would have been able to afford a top education in the United States.

FINANCIAL AID FROM UNIVERSITIES

Most U.S. colleges offer financial aid under three main categories: grants, loans, and work-study programs. Grants, just another term for scholarships, are a gift from the university: they provide financial assistance that does not have to be repaid to the institution. Students may receive grants to cover a variety of college costs such as tuition, accommodation in student housing, and meals. This is undoubtedly the best form of financial aid.

Some colleges also offer students the opportunity to borrow money directly from the institution. Although this kind of financial aid is obviously not as attractive as grants, college loans are usually a much better option than loans from private financial institutions and even the government. Private loans especially tend to offer less favorable terms such as higher interest rates. (Harvard, for example, expects students to graduate free of debt, and most do, but the university still has its own loan program for families that wish to lower the amount of their contribution during the college years.) Finally, colleges may offer students the option to work part-time during their studies and use their wages to pay for the cost of their education.

In order to become eligible for this aid, students must follow a series of steps:

1. Fill out the Free Application for Federal Student Aid (FAFSA) at www.fafsa.ed.gov. As the name suggests, FAFSA is a free form that collects information about a student's financial need based on family size, income, assets, and other characteristics. This information is then used to determine the Expected Family Contribution (EFC), the U.S. Department of Education term for the amount of money the student's family can devote to pay for one year of college. The EFC is then sent to the student's target colleges so they can take it into consideration to design the student's financial package. FAFSA submission deadlines vary across universities, but the form can be sent any time after January 1.

It is to families' best advantage to submit FAFSA as early as possible. Given that a good portion of federal aid is awarded on a first-come, first-served basis, submitting an early FAFSA maximizes a student's chances of getting a generous financial aid offer.

Tip: The College Board website provides an EFC Calculator that allows students at any point in high school to estimate how much they will actually have to pay colleges. It is useful to visit both the EFC Calculator and colleges' individual Net Price Calculator before senior year to estimate the affordability of potential target colleges and the amount of financial aid needed.

2. Fill out universities' individual financial aid applications. Besides FAFSA, different universities may request applicants to fill specific financial aid application forms, which students may find on the universities' official financial aid website for undergraduate students. These forms usually include the College Board CSS/Financial Aid PROFILE, which families with low incomes and limited assets can submit at no cost. (The College Board automatically waives its regular fee for these families based on the information about their finances provided in the form.)

Universities' official websites also contain information about specific grants that may be available for students who meet certain academic or extracurricular criteria, as well as applications for other forms of financial aid such as funds to purchase computers.

Tip: Many universities give students the choice to fill out the paper version of the CSS Profile, which can be mailed or faxed at no cost. Even if a university does not publish this option on its website, interested students should write to the admissions or financial aid office and ask directly.

3. Fill out state financial aid forms. Some universities require applicants to submit applications for financial aid provided by their home states. Students should check through their state's Department of Education which kinds of financial aid programs are available for prospective college students, especially if students are applying to universities in their home state. The National Association of Student Financial Aid Administrators (NASFAA) also provides a helpful list of financial aid programs by state.

Tip: Some students and their families are reluctant to fill financial aid forms for fear of disclosing information they deem too private. Although entering the information requested is voluntary, omitting some or all of it may result in the inability to obtain financial aid, or at least a delay in the process. In turn, delaying the submission of financial aid forms may signal lack of interest in the target college.

High school students should explore each one of the previous steps no later than the summer before their senior year. Anticipating the specific information they will have to submit will allow them to save a lot of time and not miss the several deadlines associated with the financial aid application process. At the same time, planning ahead may prompt families to start saving to pay the difference between universities' net prices and the expected amount of external financial aid, as well as take advantage of tuition prepayment discounts available at some institutions.

The help of parents or other legal guardians during this process is critical. In order to qualify for aid, students who classify as "dependents" on their parents or legal guardians will have to submit the family's income tax return and other complex financial information that may be difficult for students to obtain on their own.

For the purposes of financial aid, universities also recognize "independent" students. These are "at least 24 years old, married, a graduate or professional student, a veteran, a member of the armed forces, an orphan, a ward of the court, or someone with legal dependents other than a spouse, an emancipated minor or someone who is homeless or at risk of becoming homeless."[1] Independent students are not required to provide their parents' financial information, and may instead submit their own.

Tip: Visit https://studentaid.ed.gov to find detailed instructions to determine a specific student's dependency status, as well as free financial aid info sessions online and in your local area. The College Board also hosts free webinars on important financial aid topics such as the steps to complete the FAFSA.

Families should keep in mind that universities hire financial aid officers who are available to answer any questions throughout every step of the process. These officers can be reached through the contact information of the university's undergraduate financial aid office, published on the universities' official websites.

Students should get in touch with financial aid officers if, for example, their family's circumstances change after the financial aid applications have been submitted. A parent's sudden unemployment, a sibling's college entrance, severe illness in the household, or the parents' divorce are just some occurrences that might increase a family's financial burden. Universities want to receive any new relevant information so they can consider expanding the student's financial aid package. That is the reason universities usually ask students to submit a new financial aid application each year of their undergraduate studies.

Most selective universities are able to provide low-income students a generous financial aid package that requires students to pay a relatively small amount of money, if at all. However, most colleges do expect students, including financial aid recipients, to contribute at least a symbolic amount as a way to take responsibility for their education. One way to meet this commitment is working during the summers or part-time during the academic year through a work-study program facilitated by the university. Another way to make money for college is to explore financial aid options outside of the university.

SCHOLARSHIPS FROM EXTERNAL ORGANIZATIONS

External scholarships, also called *outside awards* or *outside scholarships* by some institutions, are grants offered by a wide range of organizations (public and private, small and large, in the United States and abroad). According to estimates, there are more than a million external scholarships available each year to high school students. And, like college grants, external scholarships do not have to be repaid.

In order to apply for scholarships, students should follow the specific instructions listed on the official communications of the organization that sponsors the award. Usually, these applications require at least an essay, one or two letters of recommendation from teachers, a résumé, and academic transcripts. While some applications take just a short time, others may take several take hours and even days to complete due to complex essay prompts and other requirements such as videos and interviews. For this reason, students should make sure they meet all the eligibility requirements for the scholarship in question, and start the application well before the deadline.

Each scholarship organization has its own eligibility requirements. Some consider students in specific locations, students of certain ethnic backgrounds, students who play a particular sport, or students who have engaged in a special kind of community service. The majority of scholarships, however, require students to have a strong academic and extracurricular record.

Given the large number and wide range of requirements of external scholarships, how do students identify the awards that represent a good match for them? The first door they should knock on is their college counselor's. These school officials are usually informed about local and national awards, and they sometimes publish them on a specific website or send them out through e-mail. Students should find out if their counselors keep a website or e-mail list, and check both frequently. The school districts' official websites often publish scholarship announcements as well.

Outside of schools and education districts, there are a variety of independent resources that also offer valuable information for scholarship seekers:

- www.collegeboard.org
- www.collegescholarships.org
- www.collegetoolkit.com
- www.collegeview.com
- www.fastweb.com
- www.gocollege.com
- www.scholarshipexperts.com
- www.petersons.com

Tip: Scholarships360 is a great source of scholarships for students in every level of high school and college. Sign up at www.scholarships360. org to receive the organization's daily scholarship notifications via e-mail.

Sometimes, the organizations students least suspect may offer their own scholarships. For example, students should check with their parents' companies, local community organizations, churches, government offices, political parties, and sports teams. Foundations, charities, and even stores and individual families may also host awards for prospective college students.

The nature of the actual scholarship also varies across sponsoring organizations. While some of the institutions may award a student a few hundred dollars, others grant thousands, and yet others include gifts such as computers and books, or an invitation to attend a scholarship reception gala.

When I received the once available Toyota Community Scholars award for an amount of $10,000, I joined about one hundred other winners from all over the country for an unforgettable all-expenses-paid weekend in Louisville, Kentucky. Over the course of two days I met extraordinary peers who had left a tangible impact on their respective communities through the most creative large-scale initiatives in a wide range of areas such as school integration and medical services.

We were treated to a tour of the Toyota Motor Manufacturing and the Kentucky Derby Museum, a cruise of the Ohio River, dance parties and a special recognition dinner attended by national leaders from the government and private sector. I still keep in touch with the friends I made during that weekend, some of whom joined me at Harvard the following academic year.

Some organizations currently host annual scholarship contests for students across the United States based on broad criteria (usually an outstanding academic and extracurricular record throughout high school). The following is just a sample of these programs, all of which provide substantial financial aid:

- QuestBridge National College Match
- Posse Scholars
- Coca-Cola Scholars
- The Gates Millennium Scholars
- Jack Kent Cook Foundation College Scholarship Program
- AXA Achievement Scholarship
- Buick Achievers Scholarship
- Horatio Alger Association Scholarship
- GE-Reagan Foundation Scholars

- Kohl's Cares Scholarship
- Nordstrom Scholarship

Given the extraordinary number of scholarships available and level of complexity of some applications, most students will only have time to apply to a small fraction. Strategically, outstanding students should prioritize scholarships with the largest potential return like the ones listed earlier.

To navigate through the application process more effectively, it is also advisable to sign up for updates from each sponsoring organization to ensure awareness of important deadlines and changes to the application. It helps to identify scholarships with similar application formats, so students can adapt previously used application materials more easily. Finally, students should not wait until their senior year in high school to apply for scholarships. Several, such as Kohl's Cares, accept applications from students in ninth through eleventh grades. There are scholarships available to middle school students as well.

Tip: Students should set up a specific time slot each week to devote to scholarship search and applications.

Many people believe that college scholarships are very limited, and that it is nearly impossible to qualify for one. As a result, many students never even consider applying to them, and many funds are left untapped. Universities themselves many times struggle to find candidates who fulfill the requirements of very generous awards.

I recently met someone who found out he qualified for an amazing scholarship from Georgia Tech only after he was already enrolled at the institution. Georgia Tech still provided him the funds, and even encouraged him to assist the staff with the search for other candidates.

Earning substantial scholarship money can make an enormous difference in a student's college experience. It means affording academic supplies, helping one's family meet burdening costs, or not having to work a part-time or full-time job that may conflict with the academic and extracurricular experiences one's attracted to. In cases where the student chooses to study far from home, scholarship money might mean not worrying about the cost of plane tickets, affording clothes more appropriate for the new climate or leading a fulfilling social life.

Through external scholarships, students may earn much more money than they could ever imagine. Take Christopher Gray, a high school student from Alabama who won $1.3 million in scholarships to attend Drexel University. Christopher, now the founder of a smart phone application called Scholly that lets users search scholarships very easily, applied to more than seventy college scholarships and ultimately won thirty-four of them.

According to an article about him that was published in Philly.com, Christopher's scholarship funds were enough to cover bachelor's and graduate degrees, including his living expenses and personal investment. Throughout college, Christopher has been able to support his single mother, formerly unemployed, and two younger siblings, for whom he has established a savings account so he can pay for their enrollment in private schools. He credits his high school grades in the A–B range, his leadership, and his service to the local community for allowing him to stand out from other scholarship applicants.[2] Ultimately, however, the key to his success was his dedication.

My own scholarship awards brought immense relief to my family. Even though Harvard had provided me a very generous financial aid package that covered almost the entire costs of tuition, room and board, my parents were hoping that we could have extra funds to purchase my flights to Boston, winter clothes and dorm and academic supplies. One of my scholarships, granted by BrandsMart USA, was effectively a voucher that could be redeemed at the store, where we got electric appliances for my dormitory. Being able to help my parents with these expenses was an amazing feeling.

Once scholarships are granted, recipients should keep a few things in mind. First, they must check whether the scholarship needs to be renewed every year, and if so, whether renewal depends on the maintenance of certain conditions such as a minimum GPA. Students should also check colleges' outside awards policy as soon as possible. Some federal guidelines and individual universities' regulations, for example, do not allow scholarship money to substitute more than a fraction of the expected student and family contribution. Aware of this policy, some scholarship organizations give the funds directly to the students so the latter may use them to cover tuition, room and board expenses, but also other costs related to college attendance.

Securing enough financial aid to afford one's target institutions is the last critical step in the college application process. At this point, all students can do is wait for colleges to make their admissions decisions and cherish what might have been an unimaginable opportunity: being on the other side of the table, where colleges do the courtship and applicants make the ultimate decision.

10

ACCEPTING AN OFFER

The Last Step in the College Application Process

Harvard had announced it would release its Early Action admissions results on December 15th. It was my longest day that year.

Despite my anxiety I was well aware of the fact that I would probably not get into Harvard. I was prepared for a rejection letter or, at best, a deferral to Regular Action, and I was okay with that. I was proud of myself for having tried. And I kept thinking of one of my grandma's many famous sayings, "stars shine with their own light." While growing up, she always reminded all ten grandchildren that our success ultimately depended on our own efforts. Our circumstances could certainly facilitate the path, but they were secondary to individual initiative. Regardless of where I ended up, I would apply the same dedication and enthusiasm to attain my academic and professional goals. And there were many good colleges, anyway. This was not the end of the world.

And yet, a letter of admission from Harvard seemed like such a far-fetched dream that I could only imagine the kind of faith that it would bring to my family. Getting into a prestigious, affordable college would be my gift to them after everything they had sacrificed to raise me.

It was well into the evening when the response from Harvard finally arrived. I logged into my e-mail account as my parents breathed on my neck, and saw the single unread message. I slowly dragged the cursor and placed it on top of the recipient's name,

Harvard College Admissions. The subject was "Admissions Decision." I finally opened the e-mail and read the first few lines:

"I am delighted to inform you that the Committee on Admissions
has admitted you to the Class of 2010 under the Early Action program. Please accept my personal congratulations for your outstanding achievements."

The excitement I felt upon reading this message could only be
compared to the moment I arrived in the United States and saw my
father again after two years. My parents were crying, still in shock.
My sister was jumping. I immediately called my grandma, in Cuba,
who also broke into tears. All of a sudden everything felt just right.

Receiving an acceptance letter during the early admissions round is
immensely relieving. At that point there is certainty that one will be
attending college, while there's still time to apply to more institutions,
with more confidence in the likelihood of acceptance. Some applicants
become overconfident and do not start working on regular action applications until after they hear back from their early round choices. When
acceptances do not arrive, the limited time available and the possible
feelings of discouragement might overburden a student completing
new applications.

I personally decided to submit applications to seven more universities, which my parents fully supported just to make sure that we
expanded our options and could compare several financial aid offers.
Luckily, I had prepared the rest of the applications beforehand, considering a possible rejection or deferral from Harvard. Given that
most of the new colleges required at least one more essay on top of
the Common Application's personal statement, it would have been
very difficult to finish on time to meet the regular action deadlines.
    By New Year's Eve I had already applied to Dartmouth, Penn,
Columbia, the University of Miami, the University of Florida,
Princeton, and Yale. Dartmouth was the first to reply in the form of a
likely letter that arrived in February, much earlier than the anticipated March and April responses. A "likely letter" is the term used to
describe the letters sent by universities a few weeks before the official decision date to communicate their intention to admit an appli-

cant. While these letters are not an official acceptance, it is very unusual that recipients are not formally admitted shortly after.

The rest of the colleges replied in the spring, an electronic message followed by print materials over mail just a few days later. Acceptances came in big envelopes full of informational booklets, letters from admissions officers and current students, invitations to visit the university, certificates suitable for framing, codes to enter social networking sites especially designed for admitted students, official university stickers, and all sorts of other exciting things. Following Yale's rejection e-mail was only a very thin envelope containing a letter with exactly the same text.

Tip: Students should not fret if they are placed on a wait list or rejected by their target colleges. Plenty of higher education institutions accept applications in the spring of senior year and even the summer; the official website of the National Association for College Admission Counseling, www.nacacnet.org, annually publishes a list of institutions that still have space available for upcoming freshmen. Students may commit to another college for the first and/or second year, and seek to transfer to a more desirable college later. They may also take a year off to work or engage in other productive activities, and apply for the freshman class in the next application round.

While there is almost too much published material on the subject of college applications, surprisingly very little has been written about what to do once admissions decisions are known. Outstanding students who have applied to a good number of colleges with a diverse likelihood of admission will normally have a few great colleges to choose from. But how exactly does one evaluate admissions offers? What are the resources available to learn more about a university before one commits to attending? And which factors could break a tie among equally attractive top colleges?

Jeffrey Brenzel, Dean of Admissions at Yale from 2005 to 2013, wrote a very compelling article on this subject that can be found on the official website of the Yale College Undergraduate Admissions under the title "Epilogue: After Colleges Accept You." Before providing concrete advice for applicants, Brenzel correctly states that "almost nothing depends on exactly which strong college admits you. Everything depends on what you decide to do once you get to a strong college, and how well prepared you are to take advantage of the infinite opportunities you find there."[1]

Once colleges release their admissions decision, it is very common for students to dwell on possible rejection letters, especially if the letters have come from their "dream" schools. Much time might be wasted appealing rejections, trying to convince the universities of the qualities they may have overlooked and which make the applicants a perfect fit for their program. Many other applicants quickly dismiss at least some of the universities that have accepted them, rushing to make a decision based exclusively on the applicant's perception of the university.

In a way that may seem counterintuitive, Brenzel advises to "wipe out every assumption you have made up to this point about the schools that have now offered you admission. Let there be no reaches, good fits or safeties. Throw away *U.S. News and World Report*. Stop obsessing over selectivity or prestige. . . . Treat all of this as a brand new enterprise and do not be hasty about putting ANY of your choices aside."

Brenzel shares that many times he has heard a student say, "I wish I had looked more closely at the schools where I was accepted. I wish I had talked to more students who went to those schools and more students who went to the school I actually picked. I really had no idea what the others had to offer because I was blinded by what I thought I knew about what I thought was my first choice school."

In the period between the moment acceptance letters are sent and May 1, considered the national deadline to report decisions to colleges, applicants will have many opportunities to engage in the careful analysis Brenzel recommends. Admissions officers and current students at the colleges will call applicants directly, offering to answer any questions about their respective institutions. Applicants will be connected to other admitted students who will also be weighing options and will offer insight into their own decision-making. Throughout this month or so the universities will court admitted students intensely in efforts to attain a high yield, the term that describes the percentage of admitted students that accepts a place at the university.

Applicants should take advantage of this time to dispel any doubts they may have about each university, contacting admissions representatives and current students as many times as necessary. At the same time, it is worthwhile to return to the list of factors of critical importance used to determine target colleges, ranking each current option accordingly.

Other factors to consider are specific developments that will take place at each university in the next four years and how they might influence the individual experience. For example, a university that is planning to expand scientific research opportunities for undergraduates through new labs or new partnerships with hospitals might be of particular interest to a prospective science major. At the same time, a university might be about to launch an entrepreneurship center or innovation contest, or about to welcome a visiting scholar in a field of interest to the student.

Tip: The universities' student publications provide great insight into student life and current academic affairs. Students should browse the publications' official websites to get a better idea about each university they are considering.

Campus visits are another great way to evaluate whether we can see ourselves in a university for the next four years. Once acceptance letters are mailed, most of the top colleges will invite students from low-income families to visit the campus at no cost, paying for plane tickets, lodging, meals, and, in some cases, transportation to and from the airport. Although universities generally welcome visits from admitted students at any point, they may host a special visiting weekend for all admits featuring an intense informational and entertaining program. Expect plenty of mixers, parties, and panels covering diverse aspects of interest to admits such as financial aid, academic departments, and extracurricular experiences.

While visiting weekends are usually a lot of fun and they give students the chance to interact with potential future classmates, attendance is not critical to make an informed decision regarding which college to attend. It is very unlikely that in just two days students will get an accurate idea of what life would be like at the given college, especially when the daily activities scheduled will hardly reflect a typical day for a student during the academic year. Some argue that it is actually desirable for admits to visit colleges on a normal school day, trying to mirror as much as possible a normal college student's schedule. Admis-

sions offices are usually happy to facilitate individual visits outside of
the official admit weekend.

*Tip: Some colleges host visiting programs on the same weekend. If so,
students may choose to attend part of each, requesting assistance from
admissions offices regarding logistics.*

> When I was considering my own college options, I had the opportu-
> nity to visit Penn and Princeton during their respective admit week-
> ends. Both visits allowed me to familiarize myself with the campus,
> stay overnight in the dorms with current students, and take part in a
> wide variety of events along with fellow admits. Those experiences,
> however, did not match the insight on life at Harvard I was able to
> get when I visited David, my mentor, during a normal school week.
>
> Attending classes, spending time with current students over
> meals, studying at campus libraries, joining private parties at the
> dorms and watching student performances meant I had a very clear
> idea of what it felt like to study and live at Harvard. Given the packed
> itineraries and the excessive interaction with fellow admits at the
> expense of quality time with current students, the usual admit week-
> ends are unable to offer this kind of realistic preview.

*Tip: It might be helpful to ask current students at the universities one's
considering why they decided to attend their respective institutions.
How did they evaluate their options? Do they regret their final decision?*

When choosing a college, students from low-income families should
pay special attention to the financial aid offers received from each institution. It is not enough to compare the amount of aid each is providing;
the composition of each financial aid package is just as important. Here
are a few factors to keep in mind when evaluating financial aid offers:

Aid breakdown

- How much of the aid is composed of grants that do not have to be
  repaid, versus loans and work-study programs?

- How much is the expected student contribution and how much the expected family contribution?

Grants

- What is the university's policy on outside awards?
- Are the grants renewable? If so, for how many years?
- Are there conditions to maintain eligibility for the grant?

Loans

- What are the loan repayment obligations?
- What is the interest rate?
- Can I get a more favorable interest rate through other loan providers?
- What is the maximum amount allowed to borrow?

Work-study

- Is part-time work required?
- What are the employment options?
- Whose responsibility is it to secure a job, the university's or the student's?
- What are the job schedules like?

Some of the answers to these questions can be found in the fine print of the financial aid documents the universities will send to recipients and their families, so it is important to read all the information presented. Financial aid officers are also available during this period to answer any question about individual aid offers, so families should not hesitate to contact them directly by phone or e-mail, or even schedule in-person visits if possible.

Tip: If a student's financial circumstances have changed from the moment the financial aid application was submitted, it is important to notify the financial aid offices as soon as possible to inquire about potential modifications in the award. Some relevant updates might include new health expenses, the loss of a household member, reduction in income, natural disasters or costs of caring for family members.

Sometimes universities with similar resources may offer the same student very different amounts of financial aid. In these cases, it is worthwhile to approach the institutions offering significantly less aid to inquire about a possible raise. Cornell University, for example, states in its financial aid website that if a student receives "a more favorable need-based aid offer from another Ivy League institution, Stanford, Duke, and/or MIT, we welcome the opportunity to match their offer of financial aid."[2] Carnegie Mellon similarly shares on its official website its "willingness to review financial aid awards to compete with certain private institutions for students admitted under the regular decision plan."[3]

Tip: Even though undocumented students cannot receive federal financial aid, they should not automatically assume that they are ineligible to receive financial aid from colleges. Many selective universities in the United States do not discriminate against this group of students, to which they apply the same need-based and/or merit-based financial aid policies they would offer U.S. citizens.

Once the admitted student has obtained answers to questions regarding academic offerings and policies, student housing and general lifestyle, financial aid offers, and other topics of specific interest such as study abroad opportunities, employment, and extracurricular participation, it is time to turn inward. Even though a student who is deciding among similarly strong institutions can have an outstanding experience at any, and even though the quality of this experience depends mostly on the student's initiative to take advantage of all available resources, the final college choice should follow careful meditation.

Can one really picture oneself happy at the college? Is there a positive gut feeling? Does one get excited upon envisioning life at the college's classrooms, dorms, libraries, and dining halls? Is one ready to embrace what might be a very different environment from what has been familiar up to now? These questions will require immense introspection and conversations with close ones—relatives, friends, teachers, and counselors—who will have the student's best interest in mind and will be able to offer advice with intimate knowledge of the student's special circumstances.

Making a final decision might be more difficult than expected, even more difficult than deciding to apply to college or going through the painful application process. At this point, a student might face issues and concerns that transcend merely advancing to a higher education level. Does one's family support the decision to attend college versus entering the workforce immediately? What about possibly leaving the hometown, or moving to a different state? On a personal and family level, what are the implications of deciding to pursue full-time studies for the next four years? What's being gained and what's being sacrificed in the short and long terms?

A few weeks before my high school graduation, when I had already committed to attend Harvard, my mother was diagnosed with breast cancer. The news came to shatter the stability our family had fought so hard to achieve since our arrival in the United States. My mother had just passed her last medical board exam and had been accepted to a prestigious pediatrics residency program in New York, where my dad was already exploring promising job opportunities and where we had already identified a good middle school for my sister. We were so excited about this new life. With my parents in the Northeast, I would be able to visit them much more frequently, and vice versa.

All these plans had to be postponed when my mother was advised to undergo chemotherapy, radiotherapy and surgery immediately. These treatments would take months, and my mother would be unable to combine them and resist their debilitating effects with the infamous rigor of first-year medical residency. Besides, my dad could not afford to leave his job now, as it provided the solid medical insurance plan that would cover my mother's treatment.

In this context, I realized that moving away to Massachusetts to attend college was irresponsible. I needed to stay to support my family, taking care of my mother in a way that my sister, then eleven years old, was unprepared to do. I told my parents that my studies were secondary, and that I could postpone the entrance to Harvard, but they were united against this idea from the very beginning. They would never forgive themselves for providing me a reason not to pursue the kind of education they had always dreamed of. My mother's sisters offered to stay with her for long periods, convincing me that she would be well taken care of, as she was. And my parents insisted that I leave as planned.

Many students will have to confront complex situations when evaluating a university's offer of admission. It might be that they feel responsible for younger brothers and sisters. It might be they are expected to work and become the primary financial support in the household. In these cases, it is essential to avoid making hasty decisions, and to discuss the whole picture, at length, with the family.

Universities themselves can provide additional information or resources that may facilitate the decision-making. In my case, knowing that Harvard would allow me to leave the school anytime to support my mother, even for long periods of time, was determinant. More importantly, the many conversations with my parents convinced me that staying behind would add to their burden and feeling of guilt, whereas the happiness of having me in college, at Harvard, would somewhat alleviate their sorrow.

Tip: Most universities allow admitted students to defer admission for at least a year, also known as taking "a gap year." Students may also apply to college after they have taken time off studies immediately after graduating from high school, sometimes undertaking professional or extracurricular activities during this period that actually enrich their college candidacy.

Although a student's decision to attend college requires careful consideration of both academic and personal factors, and although this decision may impact other people, only the student is ultimately responsible for choosing which college to attend. After this choice is made, deliberately, supported by prolonged and pragmatic thinking, the student will have reached a major milestone in life. For a lot of people, it may in fact be their first important decision.

A place at a dream college is the greatest reward for the hard workers, the disciplined, the zealous, the intellectuals, the dreamers. It is a gift that entails privileged access to knowledge, networks, and resources that in turn carry an extraordinary responsibility: to use this knowledge, these networks, these resources to contribute to society in one way or another. College is by no means a final destination. It is the best period that will offer growth and wisdom to become productive and fulfilled citizens in the United States and the world at large.

APPENDIX

Convinced It's Possible? College Preparation Timelines and Resources

If you have read the ten chapters of this book, you should have no doubt that every talented low-income student can truly afford and aspire to be accepted at the best colleges in the United States. You should also have a good understanding of the kind of students sought by admissions offices at selective universities, as well as the strategies to develop strong academic and extracurricular profiles. At this point every dedicated reader should be knowledgeable about how to craft the ideal target college list, as well as navigate the admissions and financial aid application processes.

What follows is a list of concrete steps that will help students maximize their chances of admission at a top university and take advantage of the academic, extracurricular, and college preparation resources available to them during middle school and high school. The steps also include cross-references pointing to sections throughout the book where related information can be found.

Middle School

Academics

- Take advanced courses in mathematics (such as algebra I and geometry) and natural sciences (such as earth and space science, and biology) at the most advanced level available
- Develop effective study habits that will allow you to tackle more rigorous courses successfully
- Read avidly, exploring a wide range of literary topics and genres
- Pursue academic interests (e.g., computer programming, foreign languages, creative writing) through online classes or community centers, if no related programs are available at school

Extracurricular Activities

- Explore and define your passions and non-academic interests in areas such as sports, arts, or community service through programs at school or local organizations

College Admissions

- Ask relatives, family friends, or teachers about their respective college experiences to start getting sense of the opportunities available in higher education
- Conduct research about the kind of education required for the career paths you may be considering
- Start exploring available high schools through visits and talks with current students, and choose the one that will best prepare you for a top college (see chapter 4 section, *Choosing the Best Possible High School*)
- Consider applying to high school magnet programs, many of which have application deadlines in December of eighth grade
- Discuss with your parents the opportunities to start saving money to pay the costs of college

High School

9th Grade

Academics

- Take rigorous courses in mathematics (e.g., honors geometry, honors algebra II, or honors pre-calculus), sciences (e.g., honors chemistry, honors physics, or AP Environmental Science), social studies (e.g., AP World History, AP Human Geography, or AP Psychology), and language arts (e.g., honors English) (see chapter 4 section, *Pursuing a Rigorous Curriculum*)
- Explore opportunities to take additional courses through online platforms or Dual Enrollment programs at local universities (see chapter 4 section, *Pursuing a Rigorous Curriculum*)

  - Begin to study a foreign language at school or through an external provider
  - Strive to maintain an A or a B grade in each class, and an academic average in the A range

Extracurricular Activities

- Explore opportunities in the high school setting to pursue both old and new interests (see chapter 5, *How Low-Income Students Can Optimize Extracurricular Participation*)
- Consider volunteering time and effort in benefit of good causes
- Look for summer enrichment opportunities (see chapter 4 section, *Pursuing a Rigorous Curriculum*)
- Explore jobs and internships (see chapter 5, *How Low-Income Students Can Optimize Extracurricular Participation*)

College Admissions

- Introduce yourself to your school's guidance or college counselor and ask about resources available to plan for undergraduate studies (see chapter 6 section, *Finding the Essential College Counselors: The Expert and the Role Model*)

- Sign up for your guidance counselor's e-mail list and general scholarship bulletins
- Explore undergraduate programs available in the country (see chapter 7 section, *Strategies to Explore Colleges*)
- Start preparing for the SAT and ACT exams (see chapter 4 section, *Preparing for Standardized Testing*)
- Continue exploring opportunities to save for college
- Apply for scholarships available to ninth graders (see chapter 9 section, *Scholarships From External Organizations*)
- Start reflecting academic and extracurricular achievements in a résumé or curriculum vitae (See chapter 8 section, *Application Requirements*)

10th Grade

Academics

- Take rigorous courses in mathematics (e.g., honors algebra II, honors pre-calculus, AP Calculus, and/or AP Statistics), sciences (e.g., honors chemistry, honors physics, AP Environmental Science, or AP Chemistry), social studies (e.g., AP Human Geography, AP Psychology, AP Art History, or AP European History), and language arts (e.g., honors English or AP English Language) (see chapter 4 section, *Pursuing a Rigorous Curriculum*)
- Build strong relationships with your teachers of core academic subjects
- Continue studying the same foreign language
- Strive to maintain A–B grades in each class and an academic average in the A range

Extracurricular Activities

- Develop leadership within your extracurricular activities and explore new interests (see chapter 5, *How Low-Income Students Can Optimize Extracurricular Participation*)
- Look for summer enrichment opportunities, including programs on-campus hosted by universities that interest you (see chapter 4 section, *Pursuing a Rigorous Curriculum*)

- Consider volunteering time and effort in benefit of good causes
- Explore jobs and internships (see chapter 5, *How Low-Income Students Can Optimize Extracurricular Participation*)

College Admissions

- Visit local colleges and attend admissions information sessions and campus tours
- Continue preparing for the SAT and ACT (see chapter 8 section, *Application Requirements*)
- Consider taking SAT Subject Tests in late spring (see chapter 8 section, *Application Requirements*)
- Maintain a continuous dialogue with your parents about college savings
- Apply for membership in local or national college preparatory organizations (see chapter 6 section, *Finding a College Counseling Expert*)
- Apply for scholarships available to tenth graders (see chapter 9 section, *Scholarships From External Organizations*)
- Update résumé (see chapter 8 section, *Application Requirements*)
- Meet regularly with your guidance counselor and ask about college fairs and campus visits

11th Grade

Academics

- Take rigorous courses in mathematics (e.g., AP Statistics, AP Calculus AB, or AP Calculus BC), sciences (e.g., AP Environmental Science, AP Biology, AP Chemistry, or AP Physics), social studies (e.g., AP Human Geography, AP Psychology, AP Art History, AP Comparative Government, AP U.S. History, or AP European History), and language arts (e.g., AP English Language or AP English Literature) (see chapter 4 section, *Pursuing a Rigorous Curriculum*)
- Continue the study of the same foreign language
- Consider conducting academic research at local universities (see chapter 4 section, *Pursuing a Rigorous Curriculum*)

- Read avidly and keep a record of the books and articles completed. Some universities might ask you to share a list of recent literature in the application forms.
- Strive to maintain A–B grades in each class and an academic average in the A range. Colleges will pay special attention to junior-year grades, especially during early application rounds.

Extracurricular Activities

- Develop leadership and scale initiatives in your extracurricular activities (see chapter 5, *How Low-Income Students Can Optimize Extracurricular Participation*)
- Look for summer enrichment programs, including university classes that may offer you college credit (See chapter 4 section, Pursuing a Rigorous Curriculum)
- Consider volunteering time and effort in favor of good causes
- Explore jobs and internships (see chapter 5, *How Low-Income Students Can Optimize Extracurricular Participation*)

College Admissions

- Take the PSAT at school
- Take the SAT and ACT in the fall, and again in the spring (See chapter 8 section, Application Requirements)
- Take SAT Subject Tests in the late spring (see chapter 8 section, *Application Requirements*)
- Discuss your college plans with your guidance counselor
- Find role models and talk to friends already in college about their experiences (see chapter 6 section, *Finding a Role Model*)
- Define the list of target colleges (see chapter 7, *How to Choose Target Colleges in Three Steps*)
- If possible, visit top target colleges, taking advantage of fly-in programs (see chapter 7 section, *Strategies to Explore Colleges*)
- Write college and financial aid application deadlines on a master calendar and set reminders
- Start writing the required college application essays (see chapter 8 section, *Application Requirements*)
- Continue saving for college with the help of your parents

- Apply for college preparatory organizations if you haven't done so already (see chapter 6 section, *Finding a College Counseling Expert*)
- Update résumé (see chapter 8 section, *Application Requirements*)
- Apply for scholarships available to eleventh-graders (see chapter 9 section, *Scholarships From External Organizations*)
- Identify academic references and make initial request for letters of recommendation (see chapter 8 section, *Application Requirements*)
- Check out net price calculators online to estimate potential financial aid (See chapter 9 section, Financial Aid From Universities)
- Sign up for target colleges' e-mail lists

12th Grade

Academics

- Take rigorous courses in mathematics (e.g., AP Statistics, AP Calculus AB, AP Calculus BC, or Multivariable Calculus), sciences (e.g., AP Environmental Science, AP Biology, AP Chemistry, or AP Physics), social studies (e.g., AP Human Geography, AP Psychology, AP Art History, AP Comparative Government, AP U.S. Government, AP Macroeconomics, or AP Microeconomics), and language arts (e.g., AP English Literature) (see chapter 4 section, *Pursuing a Rigorous Curriculum*)
- Continue the study of the same foreign language
- Strive to maintain A–B grades in each class and an academic average in the A range, even after submission of college applications!

Extracurricular Activities

- Develop leadership and scale initiatives within your extracurricular activities (see chapter 5 section, *Scaling Your Initiative*)
- Reach out to individual or institutional authorities that could support your projects
- Explore national or international conferences in your extracurricular areas
- Participate in contests that reward your extracurricular skills and achievement

College Admissions

Year-round

- Meet regularly with your college counselor and role models
- Attend local events hosted by target colleges
- Add admissions offices' e-mail addresses to your e-mail contacts list and check both your inbox and spam folders regularly

Fall-Winter

- Consider applying to college via Early Action or Early Decision (see chapter 8 section, *Application Timeline*)
- Fill out college application forms (see chapter 8 section, *Application Requirements*)
- Request transcripts and letters of recommendation (see chapter 8 section, *Application Requirements*)
- Prepare for college interviews (see chapter 8 section, *Application Requirements*)
- Revise college application essays with the help of teachers and counselors
- Request college application fee waivers (see chapter 8 section, *Application Requirements*)
- Organize application materials for each college in different computer folders
- Update resume and share it with colleges that accept it (see chapter 8 section, *Application Requirements*)
- Consider sending supplemental materials to colleges (see chapter 8 section, *Application Requirements*)
- Send colleges the school report or profile (see chapter 8 section, *Application Requirements*)
- Notify colleges if you do not receive an e-mail acknowledging receipt of your application
- Apply for universities' financial aid and available merit scholarships (see chapter 9 section, *Financial Aid From Universities*)
- Apply for state and federal aid
- Submit CSS Profile and FAFSA to target colleges (see chapter 9, *Securing Financial Aid to Pay for College*)

- Send official reports of standardized test scores to colleges (see chapter 8 section, *Application Requirements*)
- Apply for scholarships available to twelfth-graders (see chapter 9 section, *Scholarships From External Organizations*)
- Consider re-taking the SAT, ACT, and/or SAT Subject Tests
- Submit enrollment deposit to university if accepted via Early Decision

Spring

- Update the FAFSA and CSS Profile with information from your most recent year tax return
- Send target colleges the mid-year school report (see chapter 8 section, *Application Requirements*)
- Share with target colleges relevant updates to your application such as improvements in grades or class rank, extracurricular achievements, and changes in contact information
- Compare Early Action and Regular Decision offers (see chapter 10, *Accepting an Offer: The Last Step in the College Application Process*)
- Consider requesting student loans, especially subsidized federal loans (see chapter 9, *Securing Financial Aid to Pay for College*)
- Review financial aid offers and discuss with your parents if it is necessary to appeal (see chapter 9, *Securing Financial Aid to Pay for College*)
- Continue applying to scholarships; many have deadlines well past the date colleges release admissions decisions (see chapter 9 section, *Scholarships From External Organizations*)
- Notify colleges of your final decision by the expected date
- Make any required enrollment deposit and confirm its receipt
- Send final school report to selected college

EPILOGUE
An Open Letter to the Dreamers

You are a student, in middle school or high school. You value education just for the sake of it, and are willing to learn something new not because it will be on the test, but because you owe it to yourself. You are confident in your ability to *really* make the world a better place. No matter where you come from or where you want to go, you know that academic achievement will both ease and enlighten your path. You are committed to reaching your potential, and you have already accomplished an important step in this journey: seeking information.

The best colleges in the country will be fortunate to have and cultivate your motivation, talent, and resilience. Yet, although you already know how to attract the attention of these institutions and afford their education, you might still doubt that their gates are truly open, hoping to reward your hard work and become part of a personal story that is already remarkable. Even when we have all the elements to believe, dreaming can still be scary. But what a universe you might discover when you dare to envision a life without boundaries.

That is exactly what I did not too long ago, as a student in middle school, on a peaceful afternoon back in my old home in suburban Havana. My mother had taken my sister to Spanish flamenco lessons and I was still in my white and mustard yellow school uniform, seeking refuge in my room, where the open windows had brought in a nostalgic autumn sunset and fresh wind. Taking advantage of this rare moment of

privacy and tranquility, I opened my journal and wrote a letter to myself
from an imaginary future.

"To the child still within me"
Life has shown me that dreams are a reality if one truly seeks them.
After an intense, almost eternal academic journey, trying to learn
something from even the most insignificant things, I hope you have
reached what I would call the top of a great mountain. A mountain at
times slippery, at times a shower of stones impeding you to move
forward, so rough indeed sometimes you would have to stop walking
for long periods, sometimes wondering if all you had walked so far
had been in vain.
I hope that you have become a woman in charge of her own life who
has accomplished every goal through her own efforts. I hope that
after years of enormous sacrifice and to your family's pride (especially your father's), you have won admission to Harvard. I hope you
have acquired more experience within your profession and that you
have started your own company, "M.C. Stars," through which I hope
you have cultivated international success (enough to place you
among *Vanidades* Magazine's list of women who have triumphed).
I hope today you are happily married to a wonderful man whom you
adore and who loves you, of Latin origin, who shares your interests
and goals. I hope you are now awaiting the arrival of your first child,
who will fill your home in Washington, D.C. with happiness.
I hope you have brought the whole family together, helping them
live a comfortable life. I hope you have helped pay your sister's
university studies, that you have finally bought your mother the famous glass house she so wanted, and, after your church wedding, I
hope you have reignited in your grandmother the faith in God. I
hope you preserve your friends from adolescence, and that you have
been able to meet the Pope in person.
I hope you can say that you have succeeded, that you have broken all
the barriers that life has set before you, and that you are stronger and
more capable than ever. I am sure many did not believe that you
would reach the finish line, but with your parents' help, and above
all, God's, I hope you are happy. Now you know that nothing is
impossible if one has faith and follows one's heart.

For any twelve-year-old from Cuba, this letter would have seemed
little more than fantasy. I was convinced that selective universities like
Harvard were reserved for the rich and the genius. Starting a company,

especially an international company, defied expectations in a country where private venture at a large scale was and remains nonexistent. Living in Washington, D.C., purchasing a house, or meeting the Pope were equally mind-boggling ideas. At the time, property sales were not allowed in Cuba, most children could not travel abroad, and, as student government president in a socialist education system, I had to balance my religious and leadership activities very carefully.

The truth is I had never deliberately envisioned the concrete goals I wanted to achieve in life. The letter was neither a reflection of refined plans nor an intentionally hyperbolic statement designed to amuse myself if I ever decided to revisit the journal. Looking back, I am convinced that I was writing while submerged in a different state of consciousness where anything, even the most extraordinary dreams, seemed attainable.

Fourteen years have gone by since that November afternoon. Today, I am a Harvard graduate, I am married to a wonderful man of Latin origin, I have lived in Washington, D.C., and I am supporting my sister through her studies at Stanford University.

An unwavering faith in *possibility* is my most treasured gift from the adventure that began with my arrival in the United States in 2002. This period involved learning English, assimilating into a completely different society, struggling with scarcity, surviving my mother's breast cancer, and coping with the distance from our tight-knit relatives back in Cuba. In these circumstances, the opportunity to attend a renowned university became a strong source of hope that would validate the fruits of my family's sacrifice and perseverance. To this day, I face new challenges through the lens of that four-year journey: if I was able to overcome the odds then, I'm sure I can do it now as well.

Today I would like to encourage you to write your own letters from the future. Dare to dream and push your own boundaries, no matter how irrational or unachievable your aspirations may seem in the present. My hope is not only that you live these letters, but that you also leave enough space in between the lines to let yourself be surprised and challenged by life.

I wish you much success and luck. Thank you for your trust.

NOTES

INTRODUCTION

1. See Caroline Hoxby and Christopher Avery, "The Missing 'One- Offs': The Hidden Supply of High-Achieving, Low Income Students," The Brookings Institution, March 2013. For the purposes of their study, "high-achieving" students are those that score above the ninetieth percentile on the ACT or the combined math and verbal sections of the SAT I and who have academic averages of A– or above.

2. Beth Potier (2003). "Hi ya Hialeah! Summers visits Florida high school on the rise," Harvard University Gazette, http://www.news.harvard.edu/ gazette/2003/03.13/20-hialeah.html, accessed August 29, 2014.

3. Ibid.

4. "Making it Possible: Financial Aid at Princeton," Princeton University, http://www.princeton.edu/pr/aid/pdf/1314/PU-Making-It-Possible.pdf, accessed August 29, 2014.

5. Raymond Pacia and Yassmin Sadeghi, "Yale reforms financial aid policy," in Yale Daily News, March 4, 2005, http://yaledailynews.com/blog/2005/ 03/04/yale-reforms-financial-aid-policy/, accessed August 29, 2014.

I. A COLLEGE EDUCATION

1. David Leonhardt, "Is College Worth It? Clearly, New Data Say," in the New York Times, May 27, 2014.

2. Sandy Baum, Jennifer Ma, and Kathleen Payea, "Education Pays: The Benefits of Higher Education for Individuals and Society," The College Board, 2013, http://trends.collegeboard.org/education-pays. Page 5.

3. Ibid. Page 6.

4. Anthony P. Carnevale, Nicole Smith, and Jeff Strohl, "Help Wanted: Projections of Jobs and Education. Requirements through 2018," Georgetown University Center on Education and the Workforce, June 2010. Page 7.

5. Julia B. Isaacs, Isabel Sawhill, and Ron Haskins, "Getting Ahead or Losing Ground: Economic Mobility in America," Brookings Institution, 2008.

6. Stacy Berg Dale and Alan B. Krueger, "Estimating the Payoff to Attending a More Selective College: An Application of Selection on Observables and Unobservables," in *Quarterly Journal of Economics* 117.4 (2002): 1491–1527.

7. http://www.jkcf.org/assets/1/7/Why_Selectivity_Matters_in_Your_College_Decision1.pdf

8. http://www.jkcf.org/scholarship-programs/college-scholarship/why-apply-to-selective-colleges-and-universities/

9. Jack Kent Cooke Foundation, "Why Selectivity Matters in Your College Decision," http://www.jkcf.org/assets/1/7/Why_Selectivity_Matters_in_Your_College_Deci sion1.pdf, accessed August 29, 2014.

2. SELECTIVE COLLEGES

1. Anthony P. Carnevale, Nicole Smith, and Jeff Strohl, "Help Wanted: Projections of Jobs and Education Requirements through 2018," Georgetown University Center on Education and the Workforce, June 2010.

2. Stephen Burd, "Undermining Pell: How Colleges Compete for Wealthy Students and Leave the Low-Income Behind," New America Foundation, May 2013.

3. Ibid.

4. Ibid.

5. "MIT Financial Aid Background," MIT Student Financial Aid Services, http://web.mit.edu/sfs/financial_aid/financial_aid_background.html, accessed August 29, 2014.

6. "Costs & Financial Aid," Princeton University Undergraduate Admission, http://www.princeton.edu/admission/financialaid/, accessed August 29, 2014.

7. Burd.

3. THE MEANING OF HIGH ACHIEVEMENT

1. "What To Do In High School," MIT Admissions, http://mitadmissions. org/apply/prepare/highschool, accessed August 29, 2014.

2. "What We Look For," Harvard College Admissions & Financial Aid, https://college.harvard.edu/admissions/application-process/what-we-look, accessed August 29, 2014.

3. Helen Vendler, "Writers and Artists at Harvard: How to welcome and nurture the poets and painters of the future," in *Harvard Magazine*, November–December 2012, http://harvardmagazine.com/2012/11/writers-and-artists-at-harvard, accessed August 29, 2014.

4. "Admissions Facts & Advice," Dartmouth Undergraduate Admissions, http://www.dartmouth.edu/admissions/apply/thinking/, accessed June 3, 2014.

5. "The Class of 2010 reaps 80 percent yield," *Harvard University Gazette*, May 11, 2006, http://www.news.harvard.edu/gazette/2006/05.11/01-yield.html, accessed August 29, 2014.

4. MEETING THE ACADEMIC ADMISSION REQUIREMENTS AT NO COST

1. http://admissions.yale.edu/what-yale-looks-for.

2. To learn more about science research opportunities available to high school students see Shiv Gaglani with Maria Elena De Obaldia, Scott Duke Kominers, Dayan Li, and Carol Y. Suh, *Success with Science: The Winner's Guide to High School Research*, Tucson, AZ: Research Corporation for Scientific Advancement, (2011), 180 pages. Also, see the website of the Archimedes Initiative, www.archimedesinitiative.org.

5. HOW TO SUCCEED IN EXTRACURRICULARS WITHOUT SPENDING MONEY

1. Harvard College Admissions & Financial Aid, https://college.harvard. edu/admissions/application-requirements/application-tips#activities, accessed November 21, 2014.

2. "What Does Columbia Look For?" Columbia Undergraduate Admissions, http://undergrad.admissions.columbia.edu/apply/first-year/holistic, accessed June 6, 2014.

6. FINDING ACCESSIBLE COLLEGE COUNSELORS

1. Catherine E. Lhamon, "Five New Facts from the Civil Rights Data Collection," Home Room, http://www.ed.gov/blog/2014/03/five-new-facts-from-the-civil-rights-data-collection/, March 2014.
2. Contact Us, Dartmouth Undergraduate Admissions, https://admissions.dartmouth.edu/contact-us, accessed 19 November 2014.

7. HOW TO CHOOSE TARGET COLLEGES IN THREE STEPS

1. Hoxby and Avery, "The Missing 'One-Offs,'".
2. Robert Morse, "Best Colleges Ranking Criteria and Weights," in *U.S. News and World Report*, http://www.usnews.com/education/best-colleges/articles/2013/09/09/best-colleges-ranking-criteria-and-weights, September 9, 2013.

9. SECURING FINANCIAL AID TO PAY FOR COLLEGE

1. Glossary, Federal Student Aid, https://studentaid.ed.gov/glossary#Independ-dent_Student, accessed August 29, 2014.
2. Susan Snyder, "College scholarships: He's got an app for that," Philly.com, June 16, 2014, http://articles.philly.com/2013-06-16/news/39994559_1_app-college-scholarships-christopher-gray, accessed August 29, 2014.

10. ACCEPTING AN OFFER

1. Jeffrey Brenzel, "Epilogue: After Colleges Accept You," Yale College Undergraduate Admissions, http://admissions.yale.edu/after-colleges-accept-you, accessed August 29, 2014.
2. "Appealing Your Aid Decision," Office of Financial Aid and Student Employment, Cornell University, http://finaid.cornell.edu/special-circumstances/appealing-your-aid-decision, accessed August 29, 2014.

3. "Navigating College Financial Aid," Carnegie Mellon University Undergraduate Admission, http://admission.enrollment.cmu.edu/pages/financial-aid, accessed August 29, 2014.

GLOSSARY

Key Terms to Navigate This Book and the College
Applications

1. ACT: An exam offered internationally that measures what students have learned in school (normally up to eleventh grade). It has five sections (English, Reading, Mathematics, Science, and Writing) and takes about three and a half hours to complete. The format of the exam consists of 215 multiple-choice questions and an optional essay. In the United States, the ACT is usually offered six times each year. Most selective colleges ask applicants to submit scores from the ACT or SAT (see definition of *SAT*, an alternative exam) as part of the application process. Although the ACT charges a registration fee, students who cannot afford it can request a fee waiver (see definition of *fee waiver*) from their high school. Students can use a maximum of two separate fee waivers, for two different ACT test dates. To learn more about the ACT and register for the exam, visit www.actstudent.org.

2. Advanced Placement (AP): College Board program (see definition of *College Board*) that offers college-level courses in a wide range of academic disciplines to high school students. Universities are attracted to students who have taken advantage of their school's AP offerings and have obtained passing scores on the national AP exams.

3. Advanced standing: Status of a student who has received credit from a university for academic courses completed at another institution. A college student in advanced standing might be able to graduate early, or skip required courses. One way students can earn advanced standing is by successfully completing a rigorous college-level curriculum while still in high school (see definition of *Advanced Placement, Dual enrollment*, and *International Baccalaureate*).

4. Alumni: Term used to describe the graduates of a given academic institution. Alumni are also known as "graduates."

5. Application fee: The cost of sending an application for admission to a university. While some universities do not charge fees, most selective institutions do (see definition of *selective universities*). However, low-income students may not have to pay application fees if they secure application fee waivers (see definition of *fee waiver*).

6. Bachelor's degree: Academic degree earned after the completion of some undergraduate programs, usually those that take at least three years (and usually four) to complete. Most selective colleges offer a bachelor's degree.

7. Binding admissions: University admissions policy that requires applicants to accept a spot at the institution if they are admitted (see definition of *Early Decision*).

8. Class rank: The order of students within the same school year, by academic average. College admissions officers look at a student's place in the class rank as a measure of academic performance. Whereas the academic average (see definition of *Grade Point Average*) indicates the extent to which a student has mastered academic material, the class rank, by definition, describes how a given student has performed academically relative to the rest. The most selective colleges usually seek students within the top 5 percent of their class.

9. College: Post-secondary academic institution that offers undergraduate programs (see definition of *undergraduate*) such as those leading to a bachelor's degree. A university might offer both undergraduate and graduate programs (such as master's and doctorates). Therefore, a college may be an independent institution or a division of a university. High school students usually

continue their education at a college, and college studies are considered university-level studies.

10. College counselor: Professional who coaches students on the college application procedures, the expectations of specific colleges, and the unique ways in which individual students can enhance their application. Typically, a college counselor is the high school official appointed to help students navigate the college application process. However, some schools do not have a college counselor, and there are private college counselors that offer college guidance outside of the school system.

11. CSS/Financial Aid PROFILE: A form accessed through www.collegeboard.com that collects detailed information about college applicants and their families as part of the process to request financial aid from target universities. Many selective universities require the submission of this form as part of the college application process.

12. Curriculum: The history of courses pursued by a student during an academic period such as high school or college. While university admissions officers consider many indicators of applicants' academic competency, none is most important than sustained strong performance in a rigorous high school curriculum.

13. Deferral: Process by which college admissions offices postpone the evaluation of an applicant to later admission rounds in the same college application cycle.

14. Degree: Postsecondary diploma granted to a student upon successful completion of a program of studies at a university.

15. Dual enrollment: Program through which a student can take courses at a university while still in high school. Many high schools offer students in good academic standing the opportunity to undertake parallel studies through dual enrollment programs, usually in partnership with local universities.

16. Early Action: A college admissions application round that closes earlier than the regular application deadline for the same admissions cycle. The universities that offer Early Action normally require students to submit applications in October or November of the year before they expect to start their university studies— about one to two months before the regular application deadline. Early Action enables applicants to receive an admissions decision

by December or January, whereas candidates that apply in the
regular round usually get a response in the spring of their last
year of high school. Candidates accepted to a university during
Early Action have as much time as regular candidates to notify
universities of their decision to attend or not.

17. Early Decision: A binding college admissions application round
(see definition of *binding admissions*) that closes earlier than the
regular application deadline for the same admissions cycle. Unlike Early Action, Early Decision implies the applicants' obligation to attend the college that accepts them under this application
round. Applicants must withdraw their applications to any other
colleges if their Early Decision institution accepts them.

18. Expected Family Contribution (EFC): Number used by universities to calculate the amount of student aid from federal government funds that the student is eligible to receive. This number is
obtained when analyzing the information that college applicants
and their families enter in the Free Application for Federal Student Aid, commonly known as FAFSA (see definition of *Free
Application for Federal Student Aid*). The EFC is not the amount
of money a student's family will have to pay for college.

19. Extracurricular activities: Enriching activities that students take
part in voluntarily besides their academic obligations. Participation in school organizations, full and part-time employment, and
involvement in community groups such as at church all classify as
extracurricular activities. When evaluating applicants for admission, universities are attracted not only to the students' academic
achievements, but also to the leadership, diversity of interests,
and community engagement demonstrated through extracurriculars.

20. Fee waiver: When applied to college applications, document that
allows students to submit an application at no cost. When applied
to standardized testing (see definition of *standardized exam*),
document that allows students to take exams without paying the
registration fees. This book explains how low-income students
can secure multiple fee waivers to save money when taking standardized tests and applying to college.

21. Financial aid: Funds granted to students to help them cover the
costs of university studies. Financial aid can take the form of

loans, grants (see definition of *grant*), or work-study programs (see definition of *work-study*). Both the universities themselves and external organizations such as the government, foundations, and private companies may offer financial aid to high school students as early as ninth grade.

22. Free Application for Federal Student Aid (FAFSA): Form required from college applicants and current college students to qualify for financial aid provided by the government, thus lowering the costs of completing university studies. The FAFSA can be submitted as early as January through the program's official website, www.fafsa.ed.gov.

23. Freshman: Student in the first year of an academic program, whether in high school or college.

24. Freshman admission: Colleges' admission program for applicants that seek to enter as first-year students. Most high school students apply to enter college as freshmen (see definition of *freshman*).

25. Gap year: One-year break from academic studies. Many students choose to take a gap year between high school and college to pursue a wide range of activities such as independent learning, professional work, community service, religious missions, or foreign travel. Colleges encourage this period of personal enrichment and many enable accepted students to defer their entrance for a year. Other students apply to college in the course of their gap year, which can enhance their candidacy as long as they are participating in enriching activities.

26. Grade Point Average (GPA): The average value of all grades students achieve in an academic period. The high school GPA is one of the factors that colleges take into consideration to evaluate applicants' academic qualities (see definitions of *unweighted GPA* and *weighted GPA*).

27. Graduate school: Program of study, such as master's and doctorate, which normally requires prior attainment of a bachelor's degree. Some jobs (in areas such as law, medicine, dentistry, and religious ministry) require the completion of graduate studies.

28. Grant: Financial aid that does not have to be repaid (also known as "scholarship"). Many universities and independent organizations give students grants on the basis of academic merit, extra-

curricular achievement, and/or financial need, making university studies more affordable.

29. Guidance counselor: See definition of *college counselor*.

30. Holistic evaluation: Method employed by many selective colleges to evaluate applicants for admission. Through this method, admissions officers attempt to form a full picture of an applicant's academic, extracurricular, professional, and personal life, including the circumstances that shed light on why students made important decisions in each one of these areas. This kind of contextual background is as important to admissions officers as the student's academic and extracurricular credentials. Differences in individual circumstances might explain why someone with good but not excellent scores gets into a very selective school, while the same school rejects another applicant with near perfect scores in the same exams. Holistically, the first person might have been a much stronger applicant even if one aspect of this person's application was inferior compared to other applicants.

31. International Baccalaureate (IB): A non-profit educational foundation that offers rigorous education to help students develop intellectual, emotional, and social skills. The IB curriculum is available at some schools all the way from elementary education through high school, and colleges are attracted to students who have successfully completed it.

32. Internship: Job training program. There are many internships, both paid and unpaid, available to high school students in a variety of areas. Students who wish to explore careers early should thus consider signing up for an internship during school recess or during the academic year. Some schools have partnerships with local employers and allow students to substitute a period of classes for the job training. Universities value internships as an example of extracurricular participation.

33. Junior: Student in the third year of an academic program, whether in high school or college.

34. Liberal arts: One type of academic curriculum (see definition of *curriculum*) offered by top universities that requires students to specialize in one area while becoming well versed in a wide range of academic disciplines such as history, philosophy, natural sciences, physical sciences, mathematics, and literature. The liberal

arts model has been praised for teaching students the creative, communication and analytical skills that enable them to succeed in any professional path. There is a misconception that universities with a liberal arts curriculum focus solely on the arts and humanities; many in fact offer some of the most famous programs in science, engineering, technology, and mathematics. Instead of liberal arts, other top universities in the United States offer a pre-professional curriculum, which emphasizes training for specific careers such as engineering, business, and law.

35. Likely letter: A letter that universities sometimes send a few weeks before the official admissions decision date to communicate their intention to admit an applicant. While these letters are not an official acceptance, it is very unusual that recipients are not formally admitted shortly after.

36. Magnet school: A kind of public school offering a rigorous academic curriculum with a focus on a particular field. A magnet school's population is not restricted to students from specific neighborhoods, and the schools usually apply a lottery-based admissions system.

37. Major: Also known as "concentration," the academic field in which students specialize during college.

38. Massive Open Online Courses (MOOCs): Distance learning classes offered online through platforms such as edX, Coursera, or Udacity, through partnerships with universities. The wide availability of MOOCs (many of which are free) makes it very easy to complement school learning. Selective colleges value high school students' initiatives to enrich their academic training through external resources such as online classes.

39. Match: A common name (along with "peer") to describe colleges at which a student has a good likelihood, though no certainty, of being admitted. Normally a university is considered a match if the applicant's academic average and standardized test scores (see definition of *standardized exam*) are on par with the median of current students at the college. Counselors recommend that high-achieving students target between three and five peer institutions to maximize the chances of admission.

40. Minor: Secondary academic specialization offered by some universities, which may be pursued parallel to the major (see definition of *major*).

41. National Reply Date: May 1, the last date on which college applicants must notify their chosen institution of their decision to attend.

42. Need-based financial aid: A type of student financial aid granted primarily or exclusively on the basis of the economic status rather than the academic or extracurricular merits of the student. Thanks to this policy, the university ensures that its limited funds are allocated to the students in most need.

43. Need-blind admission: University admissions policy through which the admissions committee evaluates applications without taking into consideration the applicant's economic status. Such policy ensures that the committee does not discriminate against students who cannot pay the full cost of attendance.

44. Net price: Difference between the total cost of university studies and the amount of financial aid received by a student. Therefore, the "net price" is what the student will actually have to pay and it is much more important than the official price (see definition of *sticker price*). Due to financial aid, a university with a higher sticker price can be many times cheaper than another school apparently less costly.

45. Non-binding admissions: Admissions policy that does not require applicants to accept a spot at the institution if they are admitted (see definitions of *Early Action* and *Regular Action*).

46. Outside scholarship: Money that students receive from external sources to help pay the costs of college. The policies governing outside scholarships vary across institutions. Some colleges, for example, will accept these awards to reduce students' expected payments only to a certain limit. If the amount of the scholarship exceeds this limit, the colleges may reduce the provided financial aid by an equal amount.

47. Peer: See definition of *match*.

48. Pre-professional: Academic curriculum offered at some undergraduate programs to prepare students for specific careers or vocational paths such as law, dentistry, medicine, pharmacy, accounting, and veterinary science. The pre-professional curricu-

lum contrasts with the liberal arts curriculum (see definition of *liberal arts*).

49. Public research university: Public institutions of higher studies with distinguished academic research activity (see definition of *research*[AU: there is no entry for research; do you want to add it?]). Public research universities place special emphasis on recruiting professors with a strong record of academic accomplishments, and tend to offer the highest academic degrees, such as doctorates. These attributes make public research universities such as University of California–Berkeley, University of Michigan–Ann Arbor, and University of North Carolina–Chapel Hill some of the top (and most selective) in the country.

50. Rank: See definition of *class rank*.

51. Reach: A common name to describe universities where students have a low chance of getting in. Normally a university is considered a reach if its admissions rate is extremely low and/or the applicant's academic average and test scores are significantly below the median of current students at the university. Counselors recommend that students choose between three and five reach colleges in order to maximize the chances of admission.

52. Regular Action: The standard college admissions application round, which normally requires students to submit applications starting in December of the year before the start of university studies. Candidates who apply in the regular round usually get a response in the spring of their last year of high school. (See definitions of *Early Action* and *Early Decision*, two alternative application rounds.)

53. Restrictive Early Action: College application option that requires students to apply to only one institution under the Early Action program, with the usual exception of public universities. Universities that offer Restrictive Early Action allow students to apply to other colleges during the Regular Action round. Some universities also allow Restrictive Early Action applicants to submit parallel applications to institutions with early deadlines for scholarships or special academic programs, institutions abroad, and institutions with non-binding rolling admissions (see definitions of *non-binding admissions* and *rolling admissions*).

54. Rolling admissions: University admissions policy under which applicants are evaluated and notified of the institution's decision in the order in which the applicants' documents are received.

55. Safety: A common name to describe universities in which students are extremely likely to be admitted. Normally, a university is considered a "safety" when current students have median academic averages and test scores significantly below the applicant's. Counselors recommend that students apply to at least two safety institutions to maximize the chances of admission.

56. SAT: An exam administered internationally that measures the skills in reading, writing, and math that students have acquired in school up to eleventh grade. The SAT devotes one section to each of these skills, plus an essay, and takes about three hours and fifty minutes to complete. In the United States, the SAT is usually offered at least seven times each year. Most selective colleges ask applicants to submit scores from the SAT (see definition of *ACT*, an alternative exam) as part of the application process. Although the SAT charges a registration fee, students who cannot afford it can request a fee waiver (see definition of *fee waiver*) from their high school. Students can use a maximum of two separate fee waivers, for two different SAT test dates. To learn more about the SAT and register for the exam, visit www.sat.collegeboard.org

57. SAT Subject Tests: One-hour exams that allow students to demonstrate mastery of specific subjects in five general academic areas: history, foreign languages, English, mathematics, and science. While not every university requires these exams, high-achieving students aspiring to the top colleges should take at least two to confirm competency in specific disciplines. SAT Subject Tests help universities determine whether applicants are prepared for particular majors and even freshman-year courses. Likewise, strong performance in SAT Subject Tests in languages may allow students to fulfill the foreign language requirement at certain colleges, or study the language at a more advanced level. In the United States, the SAT is usually offered at least seven times each year. Although the SAT Subject Tests charge a registration fee, students who cannot afford it can request a fee waiver (see definition of *fee waiver*) from their high school. Students can use a maximum of two separate fee waivers, for two different

SAT Subject Test dates. Students are allowed to take up to three Subject Tests per test date. To learn more about the SAT Subject Tests and register for the exam, visit www.sat.collegeboard.org

58. Scholarship: See definition of *grant*.

59. Selective universities: Institutions of higher studies that accept only students that meet established admissions criteria.

60. Senior: Student in the final year of an academic program, whether in high school or college.

61. Sophomore: Student in the second year of an academic program, whether in high school or college.

62. Standardized exam: A test that is administered uniformly among all test-takers. In the context of college admissions, the SAT, ACT, and SAT Subject Tests all classify as standardized exams (see definition of each test). Most selective universities require applicants to take at least one standardized exam. The scores are used to evaluate the academic aptitude of applicants from all around the world.

63. Sticker price: Official total cost of attending a university, not taking into account financial aid.

64. Transcript: Official document provided by an academic institution listing the courses taken and grades received by a student during a certain time period. Colleges request applicants to submit high school transcripts as part of the application process.

65. Tuition: The sum of money charged by universities for their academic instruction services. Tuition is one component of the total cost of attending a university, which may include other expenses such as accommodation, meals, and textbooks.

66. Undergraduate: Term associated with higher studies programs beyond the high school period, such as those leading to a bachelor's degree. It is also the word used to describe students enrolled in these programs.

67. Unweighted GPA: Average of all final course grades received in high school based on the official scale, with 4.0 usually being the maximum. (See definition of *Grade Point Average*)

68. University: Post-secondary academic institution that may offer both undergraduate (see definition of *undergraduate*) and graduate programs such as master's and doctorates (see definition of

graduate school). Universities that offer only undergraduate programs are referred to as "colleges."

69. Wait list: Admissions policy that offers select applicants an opportunity for admission if spots in the entering class open later.

70. Weighted GPA: Average of all final course grades received in high school based on a scale that gives more weight to advanced courses such as honors, Advanced Placement and International Baccalaureate (see definitions of *Grade Point Average, Advanced Placement*, and *International Baccalaureate*).

71. Work-study: Form of financial aid through which universities offer students the option to work part-time during their studies and use their wages to pay for the cost of their education.

INDEX

academics: in 9th grade, for college preparation, 121; in 10th grade, for college preparation, 122; in 11th grade, for college preparation, 123–124; in 12th grade, for college preparation, 125; in middle school, 120

academics, in college selection process: advising for, 65; classmates in, 65; concentrations as, 64; course offerings as, 65; curriculum as, 64; faculty and, 65; graduate school and, 66; legitimacy of, 67; libraries for, 67; research in, 65–66; study abroad as, 66

academic skill, for admission: advanced high-school courses as, 20; class rank as, 20–21; as college preparation, 19; as criteria, 22; GPA as, 20, 21; high-school performance as, 19; standardized tests as, 21; summary of, 21–22

acceptance notification, 109–110

accommodation, for college selection, 70

ACT. *See* American College Testing

admissions: accomplishment meaning for, 18; class composition and, 16; contextual background in, 16; criteria for, at Harvard, 16, 17–18; decisions of, 111–118; elements of, 77–78; elimination in, 15; fees for, 78; finances and, 26; formula for, 15; good candidates for, 15; holistic evaluation for, 15–19; individual circumstances in, 16; likelihood of, 61–63; metrics for, 19–26; officers of, 15–16; test scores in, 16; timeline of, 77. *See also* extracurricular participation, for admissions; interviews, for admission

admissions decisions: campus visits for, 113–114; consideration for, 116–117; evaluation of, 111; factors in, 113; family in, 117–118; gap year in, 118; resources for, 112–113, 118; significance of, 118

admissions likelihood: athletics in, 62, 62–63; high school relationship for, 62, 63; legacy status in, 62

admissions officers, 15–16

advanced high-school courses: AP as, 19; honors as, 19; IB as, 19

Advanced Placement (AP) courses, 19

advising, 65

affordability, xvii–xix, 10–11

affordability policies, at selective colleges, 10; full financial aid as, 11; need-based financial aid as, 10; need-blind admission as, 10; no-loan policy as, 11

alternative college application support: college admissions as, 53–54; counselors as, 53; deadlines for, 52; internet as, 54; prep programs as, 52

alumni, 68

American College Testing (ACT): criticism of, 21; Hispanic students and, 47; SAT compared to, 80; score reports for, 82–83; as standardized test, 21. *See also* standardized tests
American Dream, 1, 3
Amherst College, 11
AP. *See* Advanced Placement
application fees: as application requirements, 92–95; college fund for, 93; as limitation, 92; reducing, 93. *See also* fee waivers
application requirements, 78; application fees as, 92–95; CV for, 91; essays as, 83–87; learning of, 78; main application forms for, 78–79; recommendation letters for, 88–89; regional, 79; school reports as, 90; standardized test scores for, 80–83; supplemental materials in, 87–88; university supplements as, 79; waiting period after, 93–94
application timeline: after acceptance, 110–111; deadlines in, 95, 96; for Early Action, 96, 96–97; for Early Decision, 96, 96–97; funding and, 98; for Regular Action, 97; schedule for, 96; selection of, 98
Apply Texas, 79
athletics: in admissions likelihood, 62, 62–63; as extracurricular for admissions, 24; in high school, 43; resources for, 63

bachelor's degree, job requirement of, 2
boarding schools, 29
BrandsMart USA, 107
Brenzel, J., 112

California Institute of Technology, 11
campus visits: for admissions decisions, 113–114; behavior during, 75; to Harvard College, 75, 114; importance of, 74; programs for, 75; questions for, 114; resources for, 74; visiting programs for, 114
Carnegie Mellon, 116
character, for admissions, 25
classmates, in college, 65

class rank, in high school, 20–21
clubs: in high school, 43
college admissions: in 9th grade, for college preparation, 121–122; in 10th grade, for college preparation, 123; in 11th grade, for college preparation, 124–125; in 12th grade, for college preparation, 126–127; inspiration for, 129–131; middle school and, 120
college application process: admission likelihood and, 61–63; economics of, 50; examples of support for, 55–57; experts on, 50, 50–54; guidance in, 49; role models for, 50, 55; selection in, 63–75; strategy for, 49–50, 51; target colleges for, 60–61. *See also* alternative college application support
College Board, 34, 37, 71, 72; EFC Calculator and, 101; fee waivers from, 92, 92–93; financial aid and, 101; financial aid webinars from, 102; Realize Your College Potential (RYCP) from, 93; standardized test reporting from, 82–83
College Board Application Fee Waivers, 92
college counseling experts: alternatives to, 52–54; application support from, 50–51; examples of, 56–57; lack of, 51; preparation from, 50; quality of, 51; scholarships and, 104
college education: benefits of, 1–2; social relationships from, 5–6. *See also* selective colleges
college preparation: curriculums for, 30–34; parental support for, 36–37; quality high-school, 28–29
college rankings, 72–73, 73; alternatives to, 73
college selection, for application: academics in, 64–67; accommodation and, 70; campus visit for, 74–75; characteristics of, 63; community in, 68–69; difficulty of, 59; extracurricular opportunities in, 67; finances of, 70–72; by lower-income students, 59; personal preferences for, 69; priorities in, 71–72; professional development and, 67–68; research for, 74; search

ABOUT THE AUTHOR

María Carla Chicuén is a young education advocate with over ten years of experience at renowned organizations such as ACT, Harvard University, the World Bank, the Inter-American Development Bank, Minerva Schools, and Miami Dade College.

Born in Cuba, María Carla moved to South Florida as an adolescent and enrolled in a large public high school in Miami. Her journey as a recent immigrant involved learning English, overcoming economic scarcity, and seeking creative resources to prepare for admission to selective colleges. Four years after her arrival in the United States, María Carla was accepted to five Ivy League universities and ultimately decided to attend Harvard after securing over $200,000 in financial aid. These early experiences fueled her deep passion toward higher education access and, especially, the achievement of minority and low-income youth in the United States and Latin America.

Over the last decade, María Carla has actively mentored individual students and young professionals from around the world, and is constantly delivering presentations about selective university admissions and affordability. To date she has guided countless young men and women to top institutions like Stanford, Brown, Yale, and the University of Pennsylvania.

María Carla graduated from Harvard University in 2010 with high honors in history, and pursued a Master's in International Relations with Merit from the London School of Economics the following year. She is currently based in Miami, where she serves as a Global Shaper in the local hub of the World Economic Forum. She has been named a

Top Rising Leader by Latino Leaders Magazine, and her articles on education have been published widely by Univision, ACT, La Prensa, Foreign Students, and other sources.